WORKFORCE AMERICA!
Managing Employee Diversity as a Vital Resource

MARILYN LODEN

JUDY B. ROSENER, Ph.D.

McGraw-Hill
New York   San Francisco   Washington, D.C.   Auckland   Bogotá
Caracas   Lisbon   London   Madrid   Mexico City   Milan
Montreal   New Delhi   San Juan   Singapore
Sydney   Tokyo   Toronto

McGraw-Hill

A Division of The **McGraw·Hill** Companies

This publication is designed to provide accurate and authoritative information in regard to the subject matter covered. It is sold with the understanding that neither the author nor the publisher is engaged in rendering legal, accounting, or other professional service. If legal advice or other expert assistance is required, the services of a competent professional person should be sought.

From a Declaration of Principles jointly adopted by a Committee of the American Bar Association and a Committee of Publishers.

Library of Congress Cataloging-in-Publication Data

Loden, Marilyn.
   Workforce America : managing employee diversity as a vital resource / Marilyn Loden, Judy B. Rosener.
      p.   cm.
   Includes bibliographical references and index.
   ISBN 1-55623-386-8
   1. Manpower planning—United States.   2. Minorities—Employment—United States.   3. Women—Employment—United States.   4. Pluralism (Social sciences)—United States.   I. Rosener, Judy B.   II. Title.
HF5549.5.M3L64   1991
658.3'04—dc20   90–44016

Printed in the United States of America

890DOC7

Preface

In the early 1970s, while working as an organization development specialist at New York Telephone, I was assigned a project that I thought would occupy a few years of my professional life. That project, to raise the organization's consciousness about gender issues and increase career opportunitites for women in management, turned out to be far more challenging than I had anticipated. It forced me to look critically at many assumptions and institutional policies I had heretofore accepted as "givens." It also challenged me to look at my own values, at relationships in my own life, and to acknowledge both the discomforting limitations and the intriguing possibilities for change.

My early efforts to understand institutional sexism eventually led me to the realization that freedom and equality must be universal conditions—or none can be truly free. Therefore, fighting all forms of discrimination began to make more sense to me than focusing only on one. Understanding and valuing all types of human diversity made more sense than acknowledging just a few.

Since then, with the help of colleagues like Tom Gordon, Judy Rosener, Larry Waller, and clients like the good people at Northwestern Bell (an organization whose commitment to diversity predated all others in the American workplace), I have come to realize the project that I began in 1972 is now an expanded, lifelong crusade. Everywhere, I see the incredible potential that diversity offers and the enormous waste of human talent that occurs in most organizations. Everyday, I am challenged to help clients see that potential and also recognize the waste. While this task is, at times, an overwhelming one, it is one I will never abandon. My associations with diverse others enrich me. My impatience with the pace of change motivates me to find new and better solutions. My determination to make a difference and to help institutions become more spirited, humane, and productive sustains me and provides meaning and purpose for my life. Most important of all, my conviction that respect for diversity is the key to solving our most pressing global problems continues to grow.

This book is the culmination of efforts that began in the early 1970s to help organizations value and manage employee diversity as a vital resource. It is based on all the ruminations, momentary doubts, and personal discoveries that have come out of almost two decades of consulting on diversity issues. *Workforce America* was born of a strong conviction that most people want to be part of the solution—they simply lack the awareness and skills to do so. It is my sincere hope that this book will provide many readers with the knowledge required to join in this crusade for culture change.

Marilyn Loden

Preface

I have always felt different. I'm a twin, and much taller and larger than my twin brother. As children, my brother, sister, and I never had a Christmas tree (because of our religion) but lived in a community where everyone else did. Our family was different from others in the blue-collar neighborhood where we were raised. We had one aunt who was a psychiatrist and another who was a lung surgeon—unusual occupations for women at the time. We had an aunt who was a farmer and one who was a screenwriter. My mother's career was raising three children and being a wife. It never occurred to me that women couldn't be whatever they wanted to be.

This belief was challenged in the 1970s, when I became an academic. After raising three children and witnessing the passage of the Civil Rights Act of 1964, I began to see how women, people of color, differently abled people, older people, gay men, and lesbians were disadvantaged by virtue of being different. Although my initial awareness began at UC Irvine where I am a faculty member, I soon realized that our campus was no different from other campuses, corporations, and government agencies across the country.

I learned that the reason women and people of color tend not to receive tenure at colleges and universities is because their research focus and methodologies are often considered "nontraditional" and, therefore, "not scholarly." This seemed to parallel the "glass ceiling" problem that existed within business and government. Everywhere, women and people of color just couldn't seem to "make it" and didn't seem to "fit." I asked myself why.

I looked for reasons but found no theories that, by themselves, explained this phenomenon to my satisfaction. It was clear that the influx of women and people of color into the American workplace was creating confusion, discomfort, and irritation that got in the way of good work relationships. The phenomenon reminded me of static on the radio—interference with communication and understanding—the source of which is often difficult to ascertain. So I labeled the phenomenon *cultural static*.

I continued my quest to learn more about the static issue by reviewing the growing literature on the complex sociopolitical forces that disadvantage women and people of color at work. Barbara Gutek and Jean Lipman-Blumen were my early teachers. It didn't take long to see that these forces are related to assumptions about competence, credibility, and the prevalence of organizational rewards systems that favor "sameness." It was also apparent that "otherness"—or being different from those in the dominant group—seemed to be a major issue that both employees and organizations were struggling to manage.

This book is an attempt to confront the complex, subjective, painful, yet fascinating nature of the otherness issue. In practical rather than theoretical terms, it makes a case for the importance of managing diversity as a vital resource in order to maximize organizational effectiveness.

It was fortuitous that I learned about Marilyn Loden when I began developing an interest in the study of otherness. I had used her book, *Feminine Leadership*, in my M.B.A. Gender and Management classes and found that her observations supported my notion of static. Thus, when we met at a conference in 1986, I was delighted to discover we shared a mutual interest in each other's work. Since then, we have become friends as well as colleagues. Our desire to share what we know with others brought us together to write this book. Working with Marilyn (and her husband John) has been a real joy. If *Workforce America* makes the issue of valuing diversity more interesting, more visible, more exciting, or more compelling to its readers, I will consider that joy doubly rewarding.

Judy B. Rosener, Ph.D.

Acknowledgments

W e wish to acknowledge the support and assistance of the many people and organizations that helped in the writing of this book. Without their ideas and encouragement, this project would have remained an unrealized goal. In particular, we express our sincere thanks to all the individuals who agreed to be interviewed for this book and the many institutions that cooperated with us in our efforts to gather information.

Among those who provided technical assistance were Greta Brooks, Diane Erickson, Susan Knight, Beverly Poland, and Naomi Smith. We thank them all for their efforts. We also wish to thank Richard Brahm, Jeff Krames, and Pat Pollok for the personal encouragement they provided during the writing of this book.

We are equally in the debt of several colleagues who helped us refine our thinking. In particular, we thank Lee Gardenswartz, Frank Quevedo, Anita Rowe, and Larry Waller who served as important sounding boards and Barbara Gutek, whose research was invaluable in helping to conceptualize diversity issues. We also owe special thanks to Tom Gordon, a friend and colleague who generously shared his ideas with us and did much to improve the clarity of the writing and thinking in this book.

Finally, for the moral support that they have always given us as we pursued this and other nonwifely projects, we wish to thank our husbands—John and Joe. In addition, we thank John Loden for his tireless efforts as an editor of this work.

ML

JBR

Contents

Introduction: Why This Book

A s we approach the next millennium, organizations throughout America are facing an extraordinary new challenge—unlike any they have confronted in the past. Analysts believe this current challenge will have a powerful impact on our future as a productive society. Yet few U.S. institutions seem adequately prepared today to deal effectively with this momentous change—the increasing cultural diversity of the American workforce. By cultural diversity, we are referring primarily to differences in age, ethnic heritage, gender, physical ability/qualities, race, and sexual/affectional orientation.

Today, the challenges and potential opportunities posed by employee diversity in the American workplace are a growing reality. Since 1970, the number of women as a percentage of the total labor force has doubled. In 1990, they constituted 46 percent of the American workforce.[1] In 1985, people of color made up 13 percent of the workforce. By 1988, that percentage had risen to 18 percent.[2] During the next decade, women and people of color are expected to fill 75 percent of the 20+ million new jobs created in the United States. By the year 2010, white men will account for less than 40 percent of the total American labor force. In addition, diversity in age, ethnic heritage, physical ability, religious belief, sexual/affectional orientation, and work and educational background are also increasing in the workplace as American society continues to become more culturally segmented.

Given the demand for increased commitment, innovation, and productivity in the global marketplace, can any competitive organization afford to ignore these changing demographics or assume they will have no impact on the way work is done? Moreover, can we assume that most employees, managers, administrators, and leaders are adequately prepared to deal effectively with increased workforce diversity? We believe the answer to both questions is an emphatic no.

To prosper in the future, we must value, understand, and better utilize our diversity in business, education, government, as well as in society in general. In other words, we must learn to manage employee diversity as a vital resource. *Workforce America* was written as a step towards achieving that goal.

This book is divided into three parts. Part I, "Raising Awareness," focuses on the impact that increased employee diversity will have on American institutions during the 1990s. It defines key dimensions of employee diversity. It also describes the assimilation strategy used in most U.S. institutions to manage diversity in the past and discusses the limitations of this approach for the 1990s and beyond.

Part II, "Managing Key Issues," focuses on specific workplace issues that must be recognized and addressed by managers and employees if diversity is to become a productive asset within organizations. It examines the negative consequences of stereotyping, garbled communication, collusion, and culture clash. It also provides specific strategies for addressing these issues and for transcending differences in order to develop a common sense of purpose that is shared and supported by all employees.

Part III, "Diversity and Organization Change," focuses on institutions and their leaders. It describes various approaches to valuing and managing employee diversity currently in use within leading-edge organizations. It identifies what today's leaders must *value and do* to assure that employee diversity is viewed as an asset and not as a liability throughout organizations. It also outlines a comprehensive, three-stage process for organization culture change in support of valuing employee diversity.

Because the dimensions of human difference are almost infinite in their variety, many people view employee diversity as an overwhelming topic. Some believe they must become "experts" regarding all important cultural differences that exist in the American workplace in order to manage diversity as a vital resource. But this is not the case.

Instead, managing diversity as an asset requires a framework for analyzing the impact of:

- Personal values, beliefs and actions

- Group dynamics

- Institutional policies, practices, and norms

on cooperation, mutual respect, creativity and productivity in diverse organizations. *Workforce America* provides readers with such a framework. Like a good pair of reading glasses, this framework can help one see many personal, group, and organizational issues more clearly. It can help identify the root causes of many organizational problems which inhibit creativity and cooperation among diverse employees. Most importantly, by utilizing the framework outlined in this book, managers and employees can develop a multicultural perspective that will enable them to value diversity in its many forms and successfully deal with a variety of related workplace issues. It will also allow them to begin to tap into a dynamic resource that is virtually inexhaustible in its variety and potential for creative new solutions.

NOTES

1. William B. Johnston and Arnold H. Packer, *Workforce 2000* (Indianapolis: Hudson Institute, 1987), p. 85.
2. *Handbook of Labor Statistics*, Bulletin 2340 (Washington, D.C.: U.S. Department of Labor, August 1989), pp. 19–24.

PART
I

Raising
Awareness

Chapter One
Diversity in the 90s

"The world in which we live is far too competitive to pass up available resources. You'll not win races for long, firing only half of the cylinders in your engine. . . . In my opinion, the only way to be competitive is to use all of the talent you can muster, no matter how it is packaged."[1]

Jack MacAllister, Chairman—U S West

The date is April 10, 2000. The place is the boardroom of a Fortune 1,000 consumer products company named Home Products, Inc. A major budget review is about to begin. The meeting has been called by four senior officers who constitute the corporate policy committee. Several executives from the marketing department are also expected to attend.

Stepping out of the present and into the corporate future, you enter the executive conference room. Ten people are seated at the long table, chatting informally and waiting for the gathering to come to order. As you scan the room, you think: "Wait a minute . . . I'm at the wrong meeting. This can't be the corporate policy committee."

Turning to leave, you notice a tall, distinguished gentleman (bearing a faint resemblance to Charlton Heston) standing in the doorway. His quiet, in-control air makes you feel certain that he is in charge. You walk over and ask him to direct you to

the executive conference room. "You're standing in it," he replies with a smile. "Who or what are you looking for?"

You explain that you are there to observe a high-level meeting of corporate officers and ask "Charlton" if he has any idea
where the event is taking place. He tells you, "Have a seat.
That meeting will begin right here in just a few moments." "But
who are all these other people?" you ask as you look around
the room in astonishment.

Your companion points to the black woman seated at the
head of the table. "The woman wearing the red and gray print
dress is Margot Jones, vice president of manufacturing. The
man seated to her left, wearing the tan suit and the gold ear-
ring, is Clark Baker, VP of public relations. The woman next to
him in the blue suit is Katherine Proudfoot. She's our vice president of finance. She's also a lecturer on American Indian history at the local university. Then there's William Gardner, the
African-American man in the pin-striped suit next to Margot.
He's the general counsel. Carl Philips, also wearing a tan suit,
is next. He's the new vice president of marketing and today's
his 30th birthday. Seated next to Carl is his boss, Eduardo Men-
doza, vice president of sales. The differently abled man in the
navy sport coat at the opposite end of the room is Bill Burton.
He's our human resources VP. The gray-haired man next to
him is Ed Dynan, VP of strategic planning. Then there's Mary
McKenzie, our president, in the green dress and all the silver
bracelets, Amy Wu, our VP of R&D, also in green, and me. I'm
Rodney Bates, Ms. McKenzie's executive secretary. Can I get
you some coffee or juice before we begin?"

"Ten senior people and only four white men!" you muse
aloud. "What kind of company is this anyway?" Without hesitation, Rodney Bates replies, "Why, your typical American
company, of course."

As we step back from the future and into the present, the
scene just described may seem farfetched. It certainly is not
typical of the way things look today in the boardrooms of
American business, in the offices of government, or in the halls
of academe. But our society is changing rapidly. Over the next
10 years, the demographics within the American workplace
will continue to undergo dramatic shifts—away from the European-American, male majority of the past towards a far more

diverse and segmented populace. This new plurality will include women and men of all races, ethnic backgrounds, ages, and lifestyles. It will include people of diverse sexual/affectional orientations and religious beliefs, some with physical disabilities, others physically able-bodied, who will need to work together effectively.

NEW MANAGEMENT CHALLENGES

Managing this increased workforce diversity is already posing tremendous challenges for U. S. organizations. No longer willing to deny their cultural identities to fit into the organization mainstream, today's employees want to maintain their unique ethnic and cultural heritages while receiving the respect and support of their bosses, colleagues, and organizations. In asking to be valued as diverse people, employees are also asserting that they can, in return, bring added value to their work.

The challenge for managers will be to replace the "cookie-cutter approach" to dealing with human differences with one that views employee diversity as a vital organization resource. To accomplish this change, managers must now develop the skills required to:

- Communicate effectively with employees from diverse cultural backgrounds.

- Coach and develop people who are diverse along many dimensions, including age, education, ethnicity, gender, physical ability, race, sexual/affectional orientation, and so on.

- Provide objective performance feedback that is based on substance rather than on style.

- Help create organizational climates that nurture and utilize the rich array of talents and perspectives that diversity can offer.

To say that diversity will pose new management challenges is a great understatement. Never before have managers been asked to consider the subtle and not so subtle differences among people as a key factor in their work. On the contrary, until now, most organizations have encouraged managers to look beyond differences in search of a universal, all-encompassing approach to people management—the "tried and true" way. If only human beings were that simple to understand and manage. But they're not! People are vastly more complex than employers have traditionally acknowledged. As employee diversity continues to increase, we are rapidly approaching the day when the tried and true methods for managing human resources will become obsolete.

DEMOGRAPHIC CHANGES

Like any significant change, increased diversity within the workforce is difficult to acknowledge, particularly among those who consider themselves to be part of the cultural mainstream. The magnitude of this change is already demanding new responses from each of us, though, we may prefer to deny its import in an attempt to maintain our own levels of comfort and to reinforce the status quo. Despite this tendency to deny the existence and impact of change, it is difficult to argue with the current demographics.

Here are some predictions about the ways in which the American workforce will change:

- Throughout the 1990s, people of color, white women, and immigrants will account for 85 percent of the net growth in our nation's labor force.[2]

- In 1980, women made up 43 percent of the total workforce. By the year 2000, they will account for more than 47 percent of the total workforce, and 61 percent of all American women will be employed.[3]

- In 1980, blacks made up 10 percent of the total workforce and Hispanics accounted for 6 percent. By the end of the 1990s, blacks will make up 12 percent of the total labor force. Hispanics will account for 10 percent and Asians another 4 percent.[4]

- In this same decade, the American workforce will continue to mature, with those in the 35–54 age group increasing by more than 25 million—from 38 percent of the workforce in 1985 to 51 percent by the year 2000.[5] At the same time, those in the 16–24 age group will decline by almost 2 million, or 8 percent.[6]

But diversity is not only increasing in the American workplace. Throughout U.S. society, we see evidence of increasing ethnic and cultural diversity in almost every community and geographic locale. Consider these statistics:

- During the 1980s, immigrant populations accounted for one third of the total population growth in America.[7]

- Currently, white men are a declining share of the U.S. population—accounting for just 37 percent of the total.[8]

- Among the top 25 urban markets throughout the United States, people of color now make up the majority population in 16.[9]

- Over the next 20 years, the U.S. population is expected to grow by 42 million. Hispanics will account for 47 percent of this growth. Blacks will account for 22 percent. Asians and other people of color will make up 18 percent of this increase, while whites will account for only 13 percent.[10]

Taken together, these changes in society and the workplace underscore the expanding role that diversity will play in the struggle for competitive and organizational success in the future. Whether one looks at diversity as an internal employee relations issue, an external consumer marketing issue, or a sweeping societal issue, these broad demographic changes cannot be ignored.

IMPACT OF THE BABY BUST

Another important change that will have an impact on the U.S. workplace in the 1990s is population deceleration. The baby bust of the 1970s will decrease the overall supply of younger

workers and intensify competition among organizations looking to recruit and hire people under age 24. As this occurs,
those organizations that manage diversity as a vital resource
will be better positioned to attract a broad range of new, younger employees who, for the first time in several decades, will be
in a position to shop around and select from many career alter-
natives.

Throughout the 1970s and 1980s, many career counselors
discouraged students from inquiring about corporate affirmative action programs, human resources management policies,
practices, and philosophies when interviewing with prospective employers. Today, this "don't rock the boat" employment
strategy is being supplanted by a far more inquisitive, comparative approach among younger people who see their career options expanding. Those prospective employers who have a
positive story to tell about career opportunities for culturally
diverse employees will be far more likely to attract the best and
the brightest from America's tightening labor pool in the 1990s
and beyond.

TEAMWORK AND COMMITMENT TO SERVICE

Recruiting and hiring will be just a small part of the organization challenge of the 1990s. Developing cooperative and committed work groups in which diversity is respected and supported will be the major task of corporate society during the
next decade.

Nowhere will this challenge be greater than in the U.S. service sector where the vast majority of new jobs will be created
and where employee diversity is already a given within most
entry-level positions. As success in the competitive service
economy continues to demand higher levels of employee commitment to quality and customer satisfaction, teamwork and
cooperation among diverse employees is becoming a basic necessity. Without a cooperative, efficient, smooth-functioning
work team, there is little hope of delivering consistent, high-
quality service to customers over a prolonged period of time.

Service businesses are highly interactive in nature. In industries such as retailing, fast foods, and banking, a complex set of

employee transactions must take place in order to deliver on a customer promise. If there is tension, in-fighting, disrespect, and a low level of trust among employees, then there are virtually hundreds of potential interpersonal obstacles in the path of delivering the organization's promise of quality service to the customer. While employee diversity offers the potential for increased innovation and creativity when it is managed as a vital resource, it can also pose a significant threat to quality service when it is not.

The real measure of employee commitment is most obvious at the point of customer contact. It is here that the degree of internal teamwork and cooperation are reflected back through the eyes of the client. Organizations that truly believe in the importance of quality service also recognize the interdependency that exists between the value they place on their employees and the way those employees, in turn, serve the customer. They recognize that one cannot address diversity in the marketplace without also addressing it in the workplace.

MIRRORING THE MARKETPLACE

Today, the diversity that exists in the labor force is a reflection of the pluralism that exists throughout society. Yet, in many organizations, this fact has yet to be acknowledged. Consider the disposable diaper manufacturer whose customer base is almost exclusively female, but whose product marketing team is all male. How close to the customer is the male team likely to get? How innovative will team members be? While consumer research can be used to identify strategic direction, product positioning, media mix, and so on, representative employees who mirror the marketplace and have real-time experience using a product can often provide more feedback about such issues as advertising impact, product improvements, and safety issues than those who do not.

Historically, many organizations have been successful marketing products to consumers fundamentally different from their own employee mix. But as the social fabric of America has grown more complex, diverse consumers have become less responsive to homogenized mass appeals.

MASS MARKET OR MASS OF MARKETS

To understand and respond appropriately to diverse consumers, businesses must speak the multicultural language of the marketplace. This often means discarding the mass market appeals of the past and, instead, learning to communicate to a **mass of diverse markets**—each with differing needs, tastes, and desires. How do organizations learn to diversify their appeals? One way is by listening to their own employees. By hiring employees who represent the spectrum of American society and then tapping their ideas, organizations can communicate more effectively with diverse customers.

As the global marketplace continues to develop, many corporate analysts are stressing the need for a multicultural perspective to compete successfully abroad. In an effort to assist employees who work and travel in other countries, many U.S. organizations routinely offer coaching and education in social protocol. The purpose of these orientation programs is to provide employees with important information about local customs and cultural differences, thereby increasing the probability of success in working within an international community. Ironically, while this same multicultural perspective is becoming even more important within the diverse American marketplace, few organizations acknowledge this need. The same issues of cultural diversity that make marketing and managing a challenge abroad exist within our own borders. As such, the impact of cultural diversity is as important here as it is elsewhere. Regardless of whether one lives and works in Bangkok or Boston, cultural diversity is playing an increasingly important part in the way work gets done and in the way consumer goods and services are bought and sold.

VIGOROUS INDIFFERENCE VERSUS VALUING DIVERSITY

Putting all the arguments in support of employee diversity aside, the issue of "how to manage diversity effectively" is *not* one that most managers are prepared to address. To those who consider themselves part of the cultural mainstream, managing diversity is not a compelling issue. In fact, in the minds of many, it isn't a management issue at all! As one male executive stated, "Why should we get excited about this issue now, when we've already learned to live with diversity in the U.S. workplace. Besides, the whole world already knows how to speak English."

Why? Because today's organizational realities are very different from those of the not-too-distant past. While most institutions employed women, people of color, lesbians, gay men, differently abled, older, and younger employees in the past, they seldom appreciated or utilized the talents and perspectives that these groups offered. Although employee diversity began to increase significantly inside corporate America during the 1970s, the response of most organizations to this important change was neutral to negative. Throughout the 70s and 80s, it was commonplace for mainstream managers to view diversity as a disruption and a liability. Consequently, many managers attempted to minimize the impact of diversity or operated as though important cultural differences did not exist among employees.

Today, the numbers of diverse workers who expect more than tolerance or indifference from their managers and their organizations have reached critical proportions—making "vigorous indifference" far less effective as a strategy for managing America's changing workforce.

By the year 2000, with the pace of change currently occuring throughout the labor force and the marketplace, merely tolerating diversity will no longer be possible if an organization expects to succeed. Instead, a comprehensive approach to valuing and managing employee differences will be required for both individual and organizational success.

CLOSING THE KNOWLEDGE GAP

As organizations continue to diversify, it is critical that managers and employees at all levels learn more about the cultural diversity that exists in the workplace as well as their own responses to people who are different. Regardless of what ethnic, racial, age, or gender group one examines, most people have serious knowledge gaps when it comes to dealing with human differences. Because of limited knowledge, fear, and resistance to change, there is a low degree of personal comfort with cultural diversity among most people. Yet, to function effectively in today's team-oriented, service-driven economy, workers at all levels of an organization must appreciate and learn to respect it. While we cannot put a price tag on the cost of *not* helping employees learn to respect and value each other, we know that the price includes lost time, opportunities, ideas, dollars, people, and goodwill.

Consider, for a moment, the personal and organizational pain that results when respect for differences is not in evidence and cultural diversity is poorly managed:

- The substantial dollars that must be spent on recruiting and retraining due to high employee turnover.

- The number of discrimination complaints that are filed due to the mismanagement of diverse employees.*

- The everyday conflicts that flare up and the tension created between co-workers over a comment, gesture, or joke perhaps delivered without malice but received as an insult.

- The deliberate acts of sabotage aimed at making co-workers who are different "look bad."

- The time and money wasted in corporate turf battles between members of different ethnic and racial groups.

- The cost of absenteeism associated with psychic stress.

- The time wasted due to miscommunication and misunderstandings between diverse employees.

- The enormous amount of personal energy and creativity that is wasted everyday on active resistance to this inevitable change.

---

*According to government reports, discrimination complaints have risen dramatically during the past two decades. In 1966, the first year records were maintained by the Equal Employment Opportunity Commission (EEOC), the total number of employment discrimination complaints filed was 8,854.[11] In 1981, the total was 165,306.[12] As of 1985, the total number of complaints had risen to 221,274.[13]

The cost of doing nothing to proactively manage employee diversity is already too high within the American workplace. Unless action is taken now, those costs will surely rise during the next decade, as the vast majority of employees encounter more cultural diversity at work without the insights and skills required to manage this new reality effectively.

INCREASED FRUSTRATION AMONG DIVERSE WORKERS

Today, there is evidence of increasing frustration among many diverse people throughout the American workplace. While few would cite their employers' traditional views on "managing diversity" as the major problem they face, many diverse people point to organizational indifference as a major source of their frustration. In a survey conducted among black M.B.A.s, "indifference" and "benign neglect" were cited by more than one third of the respondents as descriptive of their organizations' treatment of black managers. "Supportive in words only" was another descriptor chosen by half of those surveyed to describe the corporate climate.[14] In a national survey of gay men and lesbians, one third of the respondents saw no change in attitudes within the American business community regarding sexual/affectional orientation during the past 20 years.[15]

In other published reports, employees state that discrimination continues to be an obstacle to advancement for women and people of color. One study that examined racial and gender prejudice among more than 12,000 corporate respondents found that four out of five blacks and three out of four women saw evidence of sex and race discrimination in the workplace. What's more, the perceptions of discrimination actually grew more intense as women and people of color advanced within management.[16] What each of these surveys underscores is the critical need for change in the American workplace. Whether you examine Harris Polls on worker morale, Fortune 500 reports on attrition among African-American executives, union work actions, or the general decline in the quality of U.S. consumer products, the arguments in favor of change and the importance of managing workforce diversity as a vital resource are compelling.

A PLURALISTIC MANAGEMENT VIEW

As many tried and true methods of managing people fall short and the cost of declining productivity and employee morale continue to mount, there is growing pressure on both individual managers and organizations to operate differently. Managing diversity as a vital resource requires a fundamental shift in focus—away from a singular view of the ideal employee towards a more pluralistic view. In order to make this shift, three essential steps must be taken:

- The first step is recognizing the enormous cultural and ethnic diversity that already exsits in the American workplace.

- The second is learning to value and appreciate the full spectrum of that diversity.

- The final step is finding common ground on which to build relationships of trust and mutual respect.

Once employees, managers, and organizations take these steps, they can begin to make use of the broad spectrum of talent and ideas that diversity represents.

This book is written out of a strong conviction that the synergies created by utilizing the contributions of diverse employees are too important to overlook. Like untapped natural resources, their value and potential can be rich in rewards—both expected and unexpected—when they are put to productive use.

MULTICULTURAL SOCIETY VERSUS MONOCULTURAL SOCIETY

Regardless of whether one sees cultural diversity as a potential threat or an opportunity, there is no denying that it is an American reality. Few nations on earth have the cultural diversity that exists within our society. Given the importance of flex-

ibility, timely response, effective communication, and increased innovation in the global marketplace, it is time to recognize this important difference as a unique, competitive
advantage!

In homogeneous societies, diversity is not a factor in creative
enterprise. It can't be. In our heterogeneous society, the potential benefits of diversity are there for the tapping. Albeit there
are often bumps on the road to successful untilization of employee diversity, too many U.S. institutions are still attempting
to win the competitive race using only a fraction of their human
resources.

Consider the U.S. microprocessor manufacturer that com-
petes with Japanese, Taiwanese, and Korean firms in one of the
world's most competitive, fast-paced industries. Literally thousands of hours and hundreds of thousands of dollars have been
spent developing new strategies to improve innovation and increase profitability. Yet, a visit to the firm's engineering design
team reveals that there is not a single woman, black, or Hispanic engineer in this important group. What's more, the majority of the men on the team attended the same university, are
about the same age, belong to the same golf club, and live in
the same suburban community.

How many similar situations exist within other organizations—where homogeneous work teams attempt to solve complex problems while the talents and cultural perspectives of
diverse employees remain unnoticed and untapped? How
many managers fail to notice the organizational norms and operating practices that seem to select and encourage some employees while they discourage and reject others of equal talent?
The numbers numb.

Today, America is stepping over an important threshold into
a far more competitive and complex future. Until now, we have
managed to survive and succeed as a corporate society using
only a fraction of the talent, experience, and creativity that exists within our organizations and our society. We can no longer
afford this costly mistake. For the first time in our history, competitive success hinges on our ability as people, work teams,
and organizations to value human diversity and manage it as a
vital resource. Not only because it is the right thing to do, but
because it is the best thing to do!

NOTES

1. Jack MacAllister, "The Necessity of Diversity," *Junior League Review*, Spring 1987, pp. 8–10.

2. William B. Johnston and Arnold H. Packer, *Workforce 2000* (Indianapolis: Hudson Institute, 1987), p. 95.

3. Ibid., p. 85; *Handbook of Labor Statistics*, Bulletin 2340 (Washington, D.C.: U.S. Department of Labor, Bureau of Labor Statistics, August 1989), pp. 19–20.

4. Austin A. Kiplinger and Knight A. Kiplinger, *America in the Global '90s* (Washington, D.C.: Kiplinger Books, 1989), p. 165.; *Handbook of Labor Statistics*, Bulletin 2340, pp. 19, 23, and 24.

5. Johnston and Packer, *Workforce 2000*, p. 81.

6. Ibid., p. xix.

7. *Statistical Yearbook* (Washington, D.C.: U.S. Immigration and Naturalization Service, 1989), p. 10.

8. "Focus . . . on the White Male Majority," *The Numbers News*, October 1989, p. 7.

9. *D&B: Donnelly Demographics* (Stamford, Conn.: Donnelly Marketing Information Services, 1988), top 25 ADIs.

10. Wilma Randle, "Some Firms Facing Facts on Workforce Diversity Dictates Major Changes," *Chicago Tribune*, January 2, 1990, p. C-1.

11. *Annual Report of the Equal Employment Opportunity Commission* (Washington, D.C.: Equal Employment Opportunity Commission, 1966), p. 58.

12. *Annual Report of the Equal Employment Opportunity Commission*, (Washington D.C.: Equal Employment Opportunity Commission, 1981), Appendix I, p. 3.

13. *Annual Report of the Equal Employment Opportunity Commission*, (Washington, D.C.: Equal Employment Opportunity Commission, 1985), p. 13.

14. Frank E. James, "More Blacks Quitting White-Run Firms," *The Wall Street Journal*, June 7, 1988, Section 2, p. 37.

15. "Gay in America"—A Special Report, *San Francisco Examiner*, June 5, 1989, p. 13.

16. Jim Schachter, "Unequal Opportunity," *Los Angeles Times*, April 17, 1988, Part IV, p. 5

Chapter Two

Dimensions of Diversity

"I am no longer willing to let any part of myself take a back seat. When I come to a table, I come with all of me to the table: black, lesbian, journalist, feminist, gay activist, spiritualist, single parent."[1]

Sabrina Sojourner, Journalist and Lecturer

As we move into the 1990s, diversity is becoming a favorite discussion topic in business, government, and academe —as well as a favorite buzzword in newspaper and magazine articles focusing on the future of America. It is not unusual to hear politicians extolling the virtues of diversity in their campaign speeches or to read about the competitive advantage that diversity offers in corporate annual reports. No matter where one looks, diversity is becoming a popular idea. But what does the term *diversity* mean when it is used to describe the American workforce?

Generally, public and private organizations use diversity as shorthand for gender and race. When diversity is referenced in articles, campaign speeches, and corporate communications, it is often used to highlight one or both of these important dimensions of difference. But employee diversity encompasses other important differences as well.

DEFINING DIVERSITY

Like trees in a vast forest, humans come in a variety of sizes, shapes, and colors. This variety helps to differentiate us from each other. While we share the important dimension of humanness with all members of our species, there are biological and environmental differences that separate and distinguish us as individuals and groups. From an objective point of view, it is this vast array of physical and cultural differences that constitute the spectrum of human diversity. From the subjective point of view, diversity is **otherness** or those human qualities that are different from our own and outside the groups to which we belong, yet present in other individuals and groups. **Others**, then, are people who are different from us along one or several dimensions such as age, ethnicity, gender, race, sexual/affectional orientation, and so on. Throughout this book, **other** and **otherness** are used as inclusive terms that refer to individuals and groups who are different from ourselves.

Primary and Secondary Dimensions of Diversity

In identifying the significant ways in which human beings differ, it is important to distinguish between the primary and secondary dimensions of difference. We use the word *dimension* to describe the properties and characteristics that constitute the whole person. All individuals have a number of characteristics or dimensions by which they are measured, and no one dimension stands alone.

For the purpose of this discussion we will define **primary dimensions of diversity** as those immutable human differences that are inborn and/or that exert an important impact on our early socialization and an ongoing impact throughout our lives. Like interlocking segments of a sphere, they represent the core of our individual identities. There are six dimensions of diversity that we term primary. Listed in alphabetical order, they are:

(1) Age.

(2) Ethnicity.

(3) Gender.

(4) Physical abilities/qualities.

(5) Race.

(6) Sexual/affectional orientation.

These six primary dimensions serve as interdependent core elements. Together, they shape our basic self-image as well as our fundamental world view. Their influence on us is both constant and profound. There is no escaping the lifelong impact of these six core dimensions.

In examining the spectrum of human differences that make a powerful difference, it is the six core dimensions of age, ethnicity, gender, physical ability/qualities, race, and sexual/affectional orientation that have the most significant impact on individuals and groups in society *and* within the workplace. Together, these six dimensions inform us about ourselves and our environment. Our global perspective is built on them. Our life experiences are filtered through them. To others, they are highly salient elements of our beings and measures of our core identity. What we see and experience throughout our lives cannot be separated from these primary dimensions because our thoughts, feelings, and behaviors are inextricably linked to them.

Secondary dimensions of diversity are those that can be changed. They are mutable differences that we acquire, discard, and/or modify throughout our lives. Most are less salient than those of the core. The secondary dimensions of diversity include but are not limited to:

- Educational background.
- Geographic location.
- Income.
- Marital status.
- Military experience.
- Parental status.
- Religious beliefs.
- Work experience.

With the notable exceptions of geographic location, income, and religion, most other secondary dimensions exert little impact on us early in life. Later, as adults, we have the power to modify some or many of them. Each secondary dimension, by itself, exerts an impact on our self-esteem and self-definition. But while secondary dimensions add an additional layer of complexity to the way we see ourselves and **others**, their presence or absence does not usually change our fundamental core identity.

The secondary dimensions add contour and breadth to our self-definition. In some situations, one or several of these secondary dimensions can exert impacts as powerful as those of the primary dimensions. For instance, some Vietnam veterans have been profoundly affected by their military experiences,

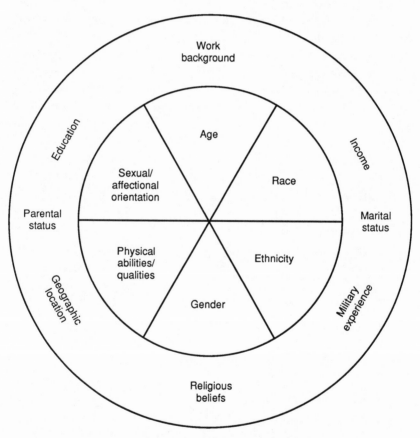

Primary and Secondary Dimensions of Diversity

while others have not been; some spouses are profoundly affected by their marriages, while others are not; most poor people are negatively affected by their income, while middle and upper-income people are not; both men and women can be deeply affected by parenthood or relocation from a rural area to a city. While situations like these intensify the impact of particular secondary dimensions, they do not diminish the primary impact of core dimensions. Instead, an additional dimension gets added to the central sphere.

The accompanying diagram illustrates the interrelationship between the primary and secondary dimensions of diversity. Typically, the central core is composed of the six primary dimensions. The secondary dimensions are additional elements outside this core—with some being quite permanent and others receding or changing over time.

Each dimension can be examined as an isolated aspect of human diversity. However, it is the interconnectedness and the dynamic interaction of these dimensions that make them so powerful in shaping our individual experiences. Taken together, these primary and secondary dimensions of diversity are key elements in our personal identities. They do much to shape our values, perceptions, priorities, and experiences throughout life.

IMPACT OF DIMENSIONS

Together, the dimensions of diversity provide us with a unique perspective about our environment. We relate to our environment and the people in it based on the overall perspective or worldview created by the particular dimensions of diversity that help to define us. We develop a particular style of communication based on these primary and secondary dimensions. The dimensions of diversity also distinguish us from **others** who possess a different world view.

Diverse Expectations, Priorities, and Concerns

Every individual enters the workplace with a unique perspective shaped by these dimensions and by past experiences. As a result, while we may work in the same office, read the same memos, and attend the same meetings, we are likely to experience the office, those memos, and meetings differently. Our diversity will also result in different needs and expectations.

As an example, let's consider two employees who work in the same organization. One is a man, age 50. He has a college degree and is an assistant vice president. He is a third-generation Norwegian-American and a practicing Roman Catholic. His two children are both adults. His wife works part-time outside the home. He is in excellent physical health.

The other employee is a Chicana clerical worker, age 29. She is active in the union local and is the mother of two children under the age of 10. A high school graduate, she attends evening classes and hopes to obtain a two-year degree. She is also a practicing Roman Catholic and a single parent. While her own health is excellent, one of her children is developmentally disabled.

Given this small amount of background about these two employees, can we predict with any accuracy the personal priorities and career expectations they may have as employees of the same organization? To what degree are their expectations, needs, and concerns likely to be similar or dissimilar? Which employee would be more likely to want an on-site day-care center; a fitness center that is open in the evenings; tuition reimbursement as a benefit; an executive bonus plan; a rigorously monitored affirmative action program; enhanced retirement benefits; supervisory training; corporate membership in a golf club; financial aid for special education?

Specific answers might depend on additional information unknown at this point. But the general importance of age, education, ethnicity, gender, physical ability, work experience, and race as factors in shaping the expectations of these two employees cannot be overlooked. The primary and secondary dimensions of diversity *do* matter. If we changed just one dimension of difference in the mix, we could expect to see a shift in the priorities, concerns, and goals of both individuals. For instance, if the woman employee described earlier was age 50 and the man was a high school graduate there would likely be a shift in worldview, personal priorities, expectations, concerns, and so on.

Humans as Complex Systems

Human beings are complex systems and each dimension of diversity adds another element of complexity to the overall functioning of the system. Because of our individual diversity, we present ourselves to the world and to each other as multi-faceted beings with a complex set of values, roles, experiences, and perceptions from which we draw meaning.

With the richness in perspectives and the abundance of human permutations that such a range of diversity offers, one would think that our human curiosity would be continuously aroused as we made our way through life and went about the business of establishing new relationships. Yet, the irony is that most of us prefer knowns over unknowns and homogeneity over heterogeneity. We prefer to be with people like ourselves. Why? In large part because it is more comfortable to be with others of a similar core identity. In choosing to relate to people who are like ourselves, the potential for interpersonal conflict is minimized while the prospect of congeniality is maximized.

HOMOGENEOUS CLUSTERING

Throughout America, most people live in homogeneous communities where they associate largely with others of similar cultural background. This homogeneous clustering is most noticeable when we look at the dimension of race. Despite legislative attempts during the past 25 years to change the racial composition of our communities and move towards greater integration, today there are indications that we are a more racially segregated society than most Americans realize.[2] And race is not the only dimension that divides us. In communities across America, we see age, ethnicity, income, religion, sexual/affectional orientation, and work background used as criteria in decisions regarding where to live. Whether by choice or out of necessity, most people in our society live in communities that are far less diverse than the society at large.

As a consequence, few of us are exposed to a broad range of human differences until we enter the workplace. By this stage in our development, we have already formed many preconceived ideas about differences or **otherness**—based on widely held myths, false assumptions, and our own rather limited, first-hand experiences.

MYTHS AND STEREOTYPES

Because of the many myths and stereotypes that we carry with us into the workplace, it is likely that we will misinterpret or devalue some primary and secondary differences when we are finally exposed to them. As a result, we may find ourselves unable to establish productive working relationships with people of different core identities.

Regardless of age, ethnic heritage, gender, sexual/affectional orientation, physical ability, or race, most of us find more comfort communicating with others of the same or similar core identity. The greater the number of primary differences between people, the more challenging the task of developing honest relationships based on mutual respect and trust.

When we add the secondary dimensions of diversity to the mix, communication, productive interaction, and openness become even more difficult and our discomfort level rises. Building productive relationships with diverse people only becomes possible after we learn to accept and value the dimensions of difference that we each represent. Without this acceptance, both the primary and secondary dimensions of diversity often serve as roadblocks to further cooperation and understanding.

ENCOUNTERING DIVERSITY IN THE WORKPLACE

Let us revisit our earlier illustration of two employees from the same company who differed in age, education, gender, race, and work background. Imagine the 50-year-old white male executive encountering the Mexican-American female clerical worker at lunchtime in the company cafeteria. Let's assume they arrive at the cashier's line at the exact same moment in time. In that instant, both parties must make a quick decision about who goes ahead of whom on the line.

If he insists on paying for his meal first, what might the woman behind him think? Depending on her preconceived ideas about people like him, she could assume he's an arrogant senior manager, a white racist, a pushy older person, or just someone in a hurry.

On the other hand, if she steps ahead of the man, his preconceived ideas about people like her might lead him to conclude she's a militant Chicana, an uppity woman, a union agitator, or a younger person with no manners. On the other hand, he might feel she is justified in stepping ahead because "ladies should always go first." Since this random incident occurred in the company cafeteria during lunch, one could argue that the negative impact of any stereotyping that took place would be inconsequential.

But suppose these same individuals suddenly found themselves assigned to work together on a task force? Now he is the manager of the committee and she is one of several support people involved.

If he interrupts her when she is answering a question during a task force meeting, will she recall the earlier cafeteria incident? If so, will this second interaction give added weight to her earlier speculation that he is an arrogant executive or a racist? More importantly, what, if any, impact will this incident have on her ability to work with him? To what extent will she be confident that this manager will objectively evaluate her contributions to the task force? Over time, how committed will she be to the work of the group if incidents like this continue to occur?

Each day throughout the American workplace, employees encounter enormous human diversity in a multitude of situations. They may face this **otherness** in their dealings with customers as well as in their interactions with co-workers. Much of the time these encounters are neutral—with no negative consequences for anyone involved. Occasionally, dealing with diversity will be positive—with all parties believing they are being treated with mutual respect. In turn, their respect for diverse **others** will increase.

There are many occasions, however, when communication between diverse people breaks down. This results in bad feelings, lowered productivity, heightened resistance, and the reinforcement of preconceived ideas and stereotypes about **otherness**. If these breakdowns become the norm, the results can be disastrous for organizations in which success in the marketplace is directly linked to productive teamwork and high employee morale.

VALUING DIVERSITY

Whether one looks at the multicultural marketplace or the multicultural workforce, it is clear that U.S. industry, government, and educational institutions can't hope to compete successfully in the future without valuing diversity and learning to manage it as a vital resource. As such, the decision to value diversity will not reflect a social, moral, or legal agenda in the future. Instead, this decision will be based on the "bottom line"—however this is defined. Not only will organizations that value diversity have a competitive advantage at home and abroad, they will also be positioned to cope more effectively with continued change. This is because diversity generates multiple perspectives regarding new business opportunities as well as more creative solutions to critical productivity problems.

As a management philosophy, valuing diversity assumes we will be more successful as individuals, work teams, organizations, and a society if we acknowledge, respect, and work with the primary and secondary dimensions of difference. This philosophy represents a fundamental change in the way most organizations have traditionally viewed and managed human differences. It is a philosophy that is inclusive rather than exclusive. It assumes that "none of us is smarter than all of us." Most importantly, it fosters a management approach that makes full use of the ideas, talents, experiences, and perspectives of all employees at all levels of an organization.

READINESS TO MANAGE DIVERSITY

If valuing diversity is a philosophy, managing diversity as a vital resource is a skill. It requires considerable knowledge, sensitivity, patience, flexibility, and training. While some institutions are developing the awareness, experience, and competencies required to manage gender and race as valued differences, most organizations are poorly equipped to manage all the important dimensions of difference previously discussed.

Yet ready or not, more managers and institutions are being challenged to respond to the full spectrum of employee diversity in their daily work. In the future, this challenge will be inescapable as more industries compete internationally and as more diverse people join the American labor force.

Given the complexity and uncertainty that each additional dimension of diversity adds to the relationship building process, it is not surprising that organizations, like individuals, have ignored most of the primary and secondary dimensions of diversity in efforts to relate to their employees. But ignorance and denial are beginning to translate into lower productivity, increased turnover, and declining employee morale in many organizations. To address these problems before they get worse, organizations must take a critical look at their internal cultures and determine what needs to change if diversity is to become a constructive rather than a destructive force. In addition, managers must also be willing to assess their personal readiness to value differences—something that many are still reluctant to do.

HISTORICAL ASSUMPTIONS ABOUT DIVERSITY

This individual and cultural assessment must begin with an in-depth examination of the historical assumptions made about employee diversity within the American workplace. How have most organizations dealt with diversity or **otherness** in the past? To what extent has diversity been valued or devalued? What traditional assumptions still influence the way in which institutions manage diversity today?

While some organizations are changing their cultures in support of greater employee diversity, most American institutions and managers continue to relate to employee diversity based on six traditional assumptions. Although these assumptions are rooted in the past, they remain embedded in contemporary organization cultures. The assumptions are that:

(1) Otherness is a deficiency.

(2) Diversity poses a threat to the organization's effective functioning.

(3) Expressed discomfort with the dominant group's values is oversensitivity.

(4) Members of all diverse groups want to become and should be more like the dominant group.

(5) Equal treatment means the same treatment.

(6) Managing diversity requires changing the people, *not* the organization culture.

Impact of History

As a result of our colonial history, most American businesses and institutions have been shaped primarily by the values and experiences of western European white men. These "founding fathers" of U.S. industry, mainstream politics, government, academe, and society were responsible for institutionalizing many of the norms, expectations, habits, behaviors, and traditions that are the stuff of contemporary organization cultures. As the architects of industry, government, and education, they created cultures that reflected their own values and experiences and that supported their priorities and goals.

One major consequence of these historical events has been the continual *undervaluing* of **others** with core identities *different from those of western European, white, heterosexual, physically able-bodied men.* Although individuals different from the founding fathers now compose the vast majority of our society as well as the American labor force, they nonetheless continue to be viewed as **others** who are outside the cultural mainstream in many institutions. This marginal positioning leads to limited career opportunities and low expectations for most diverse people.

Much of the federal litigation of the late 1960s and 1970s was aimed at increasing the presence of diverse people—those outside the dominant group with respect to the primary dimensions of ethnicity, gender, physical ability, and race—in "non-traditional" jobs throughout the American workplace. Such nontraditional jobs included the vast majority of executive and professional positions, as well as male-dominated occupations in many technical fields.

As a result of early civil rights law enforcement, we now see diverse people in many places where none were encouraged to go before. However, while equal employment law has increased the presence of diverse people in nontraditional jobs, in most instances it has not substantially strengthened their individual power or their collective voice. While they are present in more technical jobs and at higher management and professional levels, they are still **marginal** in many respects. Why? Because most organizations and managers continue to operate under the false assumption that **otherness** is a liability rather than an important asset.

Otherness as a Deficiency

Although it has been more than 25 years since the passage of civil rights legislation in the United States, there remains much conflict and controversy surrounding affirmative action in the American workplace. At the heart of this debate is the historical fact that equal employment opportunity was imposed by government fiat rather than self-initiated. In the vast majority of U.S. organizations, it was a forced change rather than a voluntary one.

The response to this forced change was grudging compliance. In many public and private organizations, the problems of employment discrimination and the need for change went unrecognized. Thus, government-imposed programs were largely viewed as wasteful and unnecessary. This grudging response to the law throughout U.S. organizations sent a strong signal to employees about the perceived value of diversity in the workplace.

In essence, this attitude reinforced the historical view that diverse people were not qualified and that affirmative action was a poor but necessary compromise. In part, this attitude was the result of a lack of understanding about the meaning of affirmative action. However, it was also due to a strong belief that organizations would be forced to compromise their standards in order to comply.

Today, while most institutions recognize that some benefits result from affirmative action, there is still widespread belief among managers and mainstream employees that those who are different are also inferior. Although many organizations refuse to recognize or admit to it, there continues to be evidence of strong bias against employee diversity among some employees in virtually all institutional settings. One would think that by now this would not be the case. But while more and more people welcome the opportunity to work with diverse groups than ever before, many continue to resist this change.

These resisters often view **otherness** as "lesser than" in relation to themselves. When expected to supervise or work with diverse employees, they begin from the negative assumption that **otherness** is a deficiency that must be minimized or, better still, overcome.

Because they lack awareness of how their own preconceived ideas influence their judgments about **others**, resisters do not readily see themselves as a part of the problem. While some are conscious of their own biases, many are not. For this reason, they focus on **otherness** as the principal problem—insisting that diversity has led to a "lowering of standards" within their organizations. Until they become aware of their own prejudices and are able to honestly appraise their level of competence in dealing with employee diversity, these individuals will often unconsciously sabotage diverse employees within their work groups.

But resisters are not just individuals with biased points of view. To a large degree, they are the products of the institutional environment in which they work. In many instances, resisters see themselves as guardians of the traditional, mainstream culture. While they understand there is no escaping the changes brought about by affirmative action, they believe their organizations would not support these changes if given a choice.

To the extent that organizations do nothing to promote the value of diversity or to diminish the negative impact of resistance, they tacitly support this problem. While most institutions in America would not openly state that they foster bias and discrimination among employees, their reluctance to take action against prejudice in action or to view diversity as a vital asset reinforces the historical assumption of **otherness** as a deficiency.

Diversity as an Organizational Threat

When entering a new work group or organization, many diverse people begin to tap into their cultural heritages and experiences to develop ideas, identify and solve problems, and, in general, contribute to the achievement of organizational goals. As they do this, they sometimes call attention to their core differences—often intentionally in an attempt to raise people's consciousness, at other times inadvertently. If they are working in organizations that do not value diversity, such an approach is likely to be viewed as disruptive and even dangerous. Employees who still assume diversity poses a threat to the smooth operation of the organization often judge as inappropriate the behavior of those who are different.

The more attention **others** call to their primary and secondary differences, the more likely it is that they will be categorized as "radical" or a threat to the status quo. Eventually, if they persist, they are likely to be sidelined or even forced out by those who fear that their "negative attitude" could spread and, ultimately, affect other impressionable employees. On the other hand, some **others** may choose to assimilate into the mainstream culture—toning down their individual differences and adopting the values, style, and behaviors of the dominant group as they do so.

Expressed Discomfort as Oversensitivity

When a diverse employee openly challenges the traditional corporate norms that often stifle diversity, it is interesting to note how many people assume the real problem rests with the person and not with the organizational norms. Mavericks are rarely viewed as challengers and agents of change in institutions that do not value diversity. Instead, they are more likely to be seen as oversensitive, or as militants and agitators who, among other things, lack a sense of humor.

When a company president uses sports and military analogies repeatedly in a speech at the annual shareholders' meeting, it is the maverick who is likely to suggest that other metaphors might be more appropriate—given the fact that many women are not comfortable with such references. When an ethnic, homophobic, racist, or ageist joke is told during coffee break, it is the maverick who will object. When there is gossip circulating throughout the office about a woman "sleeping her way to the top," it is the maverick who questions the accuracy of the rumor. And each time this occurs, it is the maverick who will be accused of having no sense of humor or of being overly sensitive. Yet it is in such settings, where diversity is demeaned or devalued, that racism, sexism, and heterosexism are reinforced.

Without the underlying valuing diversity philosophy firmly embedded in an organization's culture, incidents such as those noted above create conflict and confusion in the workplace. Some employees may insist that it is their right to tell racist jokes. Those who disagree may be accused of trying to "legislate morality." There is often much debate among employees about **intentionality**—whether or not a demeaning comment or action not intended as demeaning can be judged to be demeaning.

In organizations with a clearly articulated philosophy of valuing diversity, such debates are less likely to occur. Instead, employees recognize the linkage between this philosophy, institutional policies, practices, and their own behavior. The organization's expectation of every employee supporting the philosophy of valuing diversity is clear.

Diversity and the Dominant Group

Another popular assumption that flows directly from the belief that diversity is a liability is the notion that all diverse people aspire to be more like successful members of the dominant group. The conventional wisdom on which this assumption is based is as follows: if white men are the people with an established record of success in organizations, then it is reasonable to assume that diverse people would want to emulate them. At the very least, it would seem prudent to do so.

In organizations that discount or ignore the importance of the core dimensions of diversity, it is generally assumed that the attitudes, style, and behaviors that help dominant group members succeed will work as well for diverse employees— who learn to use them properly. To assist in this learning process, many institutions counsel **others** to invest in assertiveness training, public speaking courses, image consultants, and even golf lessons in order to bridge the gap.

But, despite their best efforts to learn new behaviors and modify their approaches, many women, differently abled employees, people of color, and members of other diverse groups discover that a perceived performance gap still remains. Try as they may, they can never quite develop what it takes for full membership in the dominant culture.

Equality as Sameness

How often have you heard a manager say, "When I look at an employee I don't see sex or color. These things don't affect me. I treat everyone the same around here." This, in essence, was the position taken by virtually all U.S. institutions and by most managers when equal opportunity was a central workplace issue during the tumultuous 1970s. Since then, most organizations have gone about the business of affirmative action with the **equality-as-sameness** assumption firmly in place.

Because equality as sameness has lead to increased opportunities for some diverse people, it has seldom been challenged by those few who succeed. Nonetheless, the assumption has created a dilemma for many other women, people of color, gay men, lesbians, immigrants from other cultures, differently abled people, and employees of diverse religious beliefs who are also expected to excel and to achieve by behaving like members of the dominant group.

Recognizing that their mere presence is, at times, a challenge to the mainstream culture, diverse employees often feel compelled to adopt a style of behavior that is foreign to their self-definitions. They often attempt to modify their values and experiences in order to "fit" and conform to the behavioral and stylistic standards of the dominant group. The enormous energy that is spent learning how to assimilate could be better spent solving problems, identifying new business opportunities, or developing new programs, but this is seldom the case. Instead, we see countless examples of diverse people adapting, conforming, delimiting their potential, losing their identities and self-esteem, and, on occasion, burning out as they try to be something they aren't.

In organizations that promote assimilation and insist on sameness, most diverse people are wasted human resources. Instead of recognizing the increased innovation and creative problem-solving potential that diversity can offer, organizations that promote equality as sameness force diverse employees to assimilate in return for limited success. Since they are encouraged and expected to behave in ways that are alien to their experiences and their individual styles, **others** frequently operate at a distinct disadvantage.

In many respects, this cultural assimilation process is like expecting left-handed people to write with their right hands because they work in cultures dominated by right-handers. While it seems like equal treatment, it isn't. What's more, it is frustrating for those employees who must suppress their identities and makes little use of the talents and creative potential that they might otherwise bring to their work.

Change the People, Not the Culture

In organizations that value assimilation over diversity, emphasis is often placed on changing the people to conform to traditional norms and performance expectations. Little thought is given to how the institutional culture might be changed so that it is more flexible, hospitable, and supportive of diverse employees. This focus on changing diverse people has created difficulties for many people of color, women, differently abled, gay, and ethnically diverse people who want to maintain their own cultural heritages as they move ahead in their careers.

For while such individuals can often maintain their diverse identities at the entry level, the **range of acceptable behavior** narrows as one moves up the career ladder. What's more, the greater the number of ones' core differences in relation to the dominant group—the more marginal one is likely to be in relation to the mainstream culture *and* the more likely one is to be viewed as outside the acceptable range.

At a time in our history when we are desperately seeking ways to increase America's competitiveness and improve the quality of our goods and services, it is ironic that employee diversity remains a largely untapped resource in most public and private institutions. Instead of recognizing the value of diversity as a competitive advantage, diversity continues to be stifled and ignored in most organizations. Instead of helping employees develop mutual respect for core differences, employers often deny that these differences exist or that enhanced awareness is needed for productive teamwork. Instead of developing and rewarding managers who are competent to hire, coach, and evaluate diverse employees, organizations are insisting that nothing very significant has changed within the workforce. They continue to assert that the old ways that worked with a more homogeneous workforce will continue to work today.

Yet, the primary and secondary dimensions of diversity are becoming more visible in the American workplace and the marketplace. As this continues to occur in the future, it will be those organizations that learn to manage employee diversity as a vital resource that will benefit the most and those that refuse to let go of assimilation as a strategy for managing diversity that will ultimately lose. Like dinosaurs unable to adapt to a changing environment, they will be doomed to extinction.

NOTES

1. "Visions of Gay America," *San Francisco Examiner*, June 25, 1989, p. 64.
2. "Worse Segregation than Was Expected Is Found in 10 Cities," *New York Times*, August 5, 1989, p. 1.; Douglas S. Massey and Nancy Denton, "Hypersegregation in U.S. Metropolitan Areas: Black and Hispanic Segregation along Five Dimensions," *Demography* 26, no. 3 (August 1989), pp. 373–91.

Chapter Three

The Dynamics of Assimilation

"When I heard a schoolteacher warn the other night about the invasion of the American educational system by foreign curriculums, I wanted to yell at the television set, 'Lady, they're already here.' It has already begun because the world is here. The world has been arriving at these shores for at least ten thousand years from Europe, Africa, and Asia."[1]

Ishmael Reed, Editorial Director—Yardbird Press

W hen we look back at our history as a society, we can easily recognize the important role that assimilation has played as a strategy for managing ethnic and cultural diversity. Within most complex organizations, underlying assumptions about the value of human diversity and past methods used to manage and deal with attitudinal and behavioral differences reinforced homogeneity. Although diversity has always existed within the American workplace, the six primary dimensions previously discussed were largely ignored in the past.

As a result, powerful, homogeneous cultures developed inside most U.S. organizations, exerting an important impact on the standards, unstated norms, and expectations set for all employees. To a large extent, these cultures were shaped by the values and beliefs of those who founded our society's most important and powerful institutions—primarily white men of western European heritage.

As is usually the case with entrepreneurs, the founders of American industry created institutions and organization cultures to support their own interests, values, and goals. Out of these cultures, there developed a widespread belief that assimilation was the appropriate strategy for managing increased employee diversity. This strategy suppressed diversity and presumed that multicultural differences were dysfunctional or, at best, irrelevant.

At the same time, assimilation reinforced the value and "rightness" of the traditional culture of those in power—the organization's founders and leaders. The result was the development of institutional cultures based on the experiences, values, assumptions, and needs of the dominant group. The term *dominant group* refers to those people with a disproportionate amount of power and influence within an organization.

Today, many U.S. institutions still support the philosophy of assimilation and continue to treat employee diversity as a liability and a threat to the stability of the organization. We refer to these organizations as **traditional** because they maintain a strong tradition of homogeneity within their cultures. Instead of expanding their institutional norms to accommodate differences, these organizations expect diverse people to blend or become assimilated into the traditional, mainstream culture.

PRACTICES THAT REINFORCE ASSIMILATION

While the process of assimilation varies in subtle ways across institutions, there are several common practices employed in most traditional organizations that reinforce the value of homogeneity. To the casual observer, these practices may be evidence of nothing more than "business as usual." They often represent "the way things have always been done" and may predate the contemporary leadership of an organization. Generally, they are long-standing traditions that employees seldom question and, instead, simply learn to live with.

Although they may not appear to be particularly detrimental, such practices have a different impact on mainstream employees—who derive benefit from the traditional culture and the decisions of the dominant group—and on diverse employees. While these practices positively reinforce those in the mainstream who come closest to embodying the homogeneous ideal, they often negatively reinforce and diminish diverse employees who either cannot or will not conform.

Among the many practices that support homogeneity, five are found in most traditional organizations. These practices include:

(1) Dominant group standards universally applied to employee performance and style.

(2) Continuous competency testing of diverse employees.

(3) Maintenance of closed communication networks.

(4) Maintenance of closed decision-making systems.

(5) Suppression of support groups for diverse employees.

It is important to note that within most traditional organizations, these practices appear to be nothing extraordinary. They are operating methods that became institutionalized more than a lifetime ago. Therefore, the majority of employees often accept them as givens and do not challenge or question them directly.

Dominant Group Standards Universally Applied

Homogeneity, assimilation, and the assumption that equality is sameness are three important tenets within traditional organizations. Together, they reinforce and reward the behaviors, values, and experiences of the dominant group. They also tend to blur the distinctions between the experiences of the dominant group and all other human experience. As a result, outstanding performance becomes synonymous with outstanding white male performance—since performance is judged by the dominant group's standards.

But while there is often much overlap, the two are not the same. To the extent that the dimensions of race and gender influence our worldview, white men develop a particular style that is based on their socialization and life experiences. That style may be similar in many respects to the styles of women and people of color but it is not the same. When it is regarded as the norm for all people, it places a burden on those who are different by forcing them to adapt in order to be more like the dominant group.

In traditional organizations, all employee endeavor is measured against the standards of the dominant group. Likewise, all employee needs are evaluated and prioritized from this perspective. If, for example, those in the dominant group believe that child care is not an organizational responsibility, then nothing will be done to meet this growing societal need. If language training for immigrant workers or job retraining for semiskilled employees is seen as a government responsibility, then these critical needs will not be addressed in the workplace. In short, it is the dominant group that sets and controls the social agenda in traditional organizations, with other groups expected to follow and conform—or disappear.

Continuous Competency Testing

Among the practices that occur as a consequence of assimilation, continuous "testing" of diverse employees is one of the most prevalent. Unlike members of the dominant group, who are generally assumed to be competent until proven otherwise, diverse employees enter most new job situations with little or no credibility. Regardless of seniority, experience, past accomplishments, or level achieved, they are routinely presumed to be incompetent and expected to "prove themselves" again and again. As one woman of color stated, "Each time I get a promotion, it's as though the slate has been wiped clean again. Gone is the recognition I earned for being competent. Once again, I'm totally lacking credibility with many of my white peers. In place of support, there is a widespread assumption that my past successes were anomalies and that this time I'll finally do what people like me do best—mess up."

In new situations or settings, where peer support can play a crucial part in one's ability to adapt and succeed, diverse people operate at a distinct disadvantage within traditional organizations. Because their **otherness** is assumed to be a deficiency, they must earn their "right" to be where they are—often with little or no assistance from peers. In some situations, they must overcome peer resistance and sabotage while they are learning a new job and adapting to a new role.

As a result of this lack of support or outright resistance, diverse employees often become cautious around mainstream colleagues and hypercritical of themselves—believing that error-free performance is what is always required. They may confuse good performance with perfection—choosing to pursue the latter. Eventually, the refusal to acknowledge mistakes as an inevitable part of growth and learning places enormous pressure on diverse employees that those in the dominant group seldom feel. They may become fearful of asking for help when they need it. Left unchecked, this pressure can result in overly cautious, risk-averse behavior and increased isolation.

Closed Communication Networks

Another common albeit unconscious practice in traditional organizations is the exclusion of diverse people from informal communication networks. Due to limited access and a lack of informal contact with dominant group members over coffee, lunch, and so on, most diverse employees are often less informed about pending changes and developments occurring within their organizations. As outsiders, they are either not invited or are reluctant to participate in informal gatherings where office politics and key corporate issues are candidly discussed.

This lack of "insider information" among diverse employees is often dismissed as a bogus issue by some members of the dominant group, who maintain that the importance of informal networking is highly overrated. But while the quality of the information exchanged may vary, there is little doubt that inclusion in the informal networking process is empowering and important to career advancement. Information about key decisions, how performance is evaluated, and what lies ahead are often revealed during informal interactions that occur over lunch, dinner, or in social settings. In the absence of current information, it is far more difficult to be confident about the future or to understand the potential impact of organization changes on personal and career goals.

Closed Decision-Making Systems

Today, in virtually every institution in America, employee diversity decreases dramatically toward the top of the organizational pyramid. For example, in a 1986 survey conducted by Korn/Ferry International among 1,600 CEOs, less than 1 percent of the total sample consisted of people of color.[2] In a similar study conducted by Heidrick and Struggles among top executives in 1987, only .5 percent of those surveyed were black and no Hispanics or Asians were identified.[3] As one nears the top, position power and influence increase. The absence of diverse people in leadership positions creates a closed decision-making system in most organizations—where key decisions affecting the lives and futures of all employees are made largely or solely by dominant group members.

In traditional organizations, it is not viewed as presumptuous for the dominant group to decide what benefits to offer diverse employees, what community organizations to support, where to build new plants and facilities, how to set performance standards, and so on. Instead, both mainstream and diverse employees expect this to happen—because it has always been thus.

Suppression of Diverse Support Groups

Throughout organizations, informal networking among employees of the same core identity can be an effective antidote to isolation and lack of mainstream support. But while such networks can offer important benefits to diverse employees, they are routinely misunderstood and frequently discouraged by traditional organizations.

Since traditional organizations assume that equality means sameness, they are uncomfortable with any mechanism that draws attention to dimensions of diversity or encourages separatism or differentiation among employees. Even informal gatherings of women or people of color over lunch may be viewed with suspicion or regarded as an indication that "something is up." In the same way, support networks are also looked on as sources of potential trouble. Because they do not recognize the ways in which diverse employees are routinely shut out or ignored by the mainstream culture, traditional organizations see no need for employee support groups based on differences in race, ethnicity, gender, sexual/affectional orientation, military experience, physical ability, or any other dimension of diversity.

Instead of viewing these networks as supportive of the diverse needs and core identities of employees, traditional organizations generally regard such groups as subversive. They view employee networks as evidence of a corporate failing rather than as a necessary step in the process of organizational change. As such, stifling the growth of employee support groups is a common practice.

By refusing access to company space for meetings, company mail for announcements, company executives as guest speakers, and so on, institutions make it clear that they consider employee networks to be renegade groups. In addition, the lack of organizational support discourages many interested employees from participating in these networks—out of fear of reprisal.

When corporate efforts at discouragement succeed, employee groups often lose their momentum. Because of the negative attention that their involvement receives, many diverse employees eventually abandon these support groups. As the groups disintegrate, some members of the dominant group may feel positively reinforced. They may express the belief that there was no need for these "special interest groups" to begin with and never recognize the active role the organization has played in suppressing their natural development.

THE HOMOGENEOUS IDEAL

To appreciate the impact of assimilation on diverse and mainstream employees, one must first recognize that a homogeneous ideal exists within every traditional organization culture. This ideal represents a success model for employees to emulate and is often used as a standard for evaluating style and performance. To discover the ideal, one must identify the qualities, experiences, and abilities that are valued, reinforced, and rewarded within the organization. What key characteristics do successful employees seem to share? What background and experiences do they have in common? Aside from the obvious characteristics of gender and race, most successful employees in traditional organizations share several other qualities, experiences, and abilities.

To create a composite of the qualities of the *successful employee*, we asked diverse people from a variety of traditional organizations to list the attributes that they thought were reinforced by their organizational cultures. Here are several of the more frequently mentioned items:

- Rational, linear thinker.
- Age 35–49.
- Impersonal management style.
- Married with children.
- Competitive.
- Protestant or Jewish.
- Quantitative.
- College graduate.
- Adversarial.
- Tall.
- Careerist.
- Heterosexual.
- Individualistic.
- Experience in competitive team sports.
- Predictable.
- Military veteran.
- In control.
- Excellent physical condition.
- Mobile.

Within some traditional organizations, these qualities and abilities have resulted in a homogeneous ideal reminiscent of Lee Iacocca—the tough-battling, plain-talking, paramilitary leader who succeeded as chairman of Chrysler. In other institutions, the ideal is more like Ross Perot—adventurer, corporate renegade, and risk-taker, or like Henry Kravis—shrewd, urbane, ruthless dealmaker. Although the homogeneous ideal varies among companies and industries, the important commonalities of race, gender, and many of the culturally prized qualities and abilities described previously cannot be ignored. As one corporate officer put it, "Like it or not, wherever we happen to work—white men come in with the same thumb print."

Although successful white men in every organization see themselves as quite diverse, to those outside the mainstream culture this select and powerful group often seems remarkably homogeneous. Is this because **others** fail to notice important individual differences among members of the dominant group? Undoubtedly so. However, by dint of their **otherness**, those outside the mainstream culture are also more able to recognize commonalities among members of the dominant group. In recognizing commonalities that exist among mainstream employees, diverse people are made more aware of their own **otherness** or lack of commonality with this group.

In many respects, the experience of diverse others in traditional organizations is similar to that of people vacationing in foreign lands. While the visitor or **other** is acutely aware of the habits and behavioral patterns of the natives, the local people are not particularly self-conscious. They pay little attention to their own attitudes and behaviors. Instead, they simply go about the business of living their lives.

One of the great ironies of organizational life is the low level of awareness of cultural norms that tends to exist among most mainstream employees. Living in a culture that reinforces and rewards one's behavior tends to obscure the negative aspects of the environment from one's view. Therefore, those who are most powerful in traditional organizations are also most oblivious to the culture's adverse impact on diversity. It is usually diverse employees who clearly see and understand the impact of cultural norms—because they are often negatively affected by them.

IMPACT OF ASSIMILATION ON OTHERS

In assessing the impact of homogeneity and assimilation on diverse employees, several issues appear to be common throughout traditional organizations—regardless of the dimensions of diversity that employees represent. To varying degrees, they affect all women, people of color, older, younger, lesbian, gay, and differently abled employees working in traditional organizations.

Because they are outgrowths of organizational practices that reinforce assimilation, these issues are constant and enduring. Regardless of occupational level, seniority, or experience, diverse employees at all levels are affected by them—although some will not be conscious of the impact.

Pressure to Conform

The most fundamental issue affecting diverse employees is the pressure to conform that is exerted by the culture. To the extent that a homogeneous ideal is reinforced within the organization, diverse employees are often encouraged by their supervisors and mainstream colleagues to adopt the behaviors represented by this ideal. Some may change the way they dress in order to fit in, others will attempt to change their presentation style to conform to mainstream expectations. Regardless of how successful these "organizational make-overs" are, **others** rarely succeed in gaining recognition and acceptance within the mainstream culture. Because their diversity is not valued or understood, most **others** continue to be viewed as lacking the "right stuff"—even as they lose touch with their own identities in an effort to conform.

The classic dilemma that confronts many women managers illustrates the point. When women enter management, they are often advised by their mentors and colleagues to become more assertive and to change their presentation style. Later on, when they learn to emulate the tough, autocratic style of many successful male leaders, they are often criticized for being "pushy" and "unfeminine."

The Presumption of Guilt

In many traditional organizations, it is common for diverse people to be both underrecognized and critically scrutinized at the same time. Because their **otherness** is viewed as a deficiency, diverse employees often receive less credit for their accomplishments than do mainstream employees. Since they are assumed to be less competent than those in the dominant group, their achievements are often misattributed and credited to dominant group members. However, in the case of errors, the opposite is true. When a mistake is made within the work group, **others** are often singled out as prime suspects. There is the presumption of guilt and the endless need to prove one's innocence. As one differently abled office worker stated, "At times, I feel as if I'm under a microscope. When an error is made in the unit, my boss always comes to me first. Then, when it turns out to be someone else's mistake—which it usually does—he acts like nothing happened. There's never an apology or acknowledgment that he misjudged me."

Role Confusion

Because **others** are unlikely to hold positions of authority within traditional organizations, those few invested with a degree of role power are often assumed to have none. In many traditional organizations, there is ongoing confusion regarding the real versus presumed role of these diverse individuals. There is also a frequent assumption made by mainstream members that diverse leaders are not what they appear to be.

A black executive tells this story to illustrate the point: "It is not uncommon for people in this company to express surprise and amazement when they find out that I'm an attorney. If they see me around the building, they assume I'm a clerk. Otherwise, they think I'm a technician or a custodian. Even though I dress in three-piece suits and carry a briefcase to work, many people have trouble seeing and accepting me as a professional."

Where there is role confusion, there is frequently stereotyping. Role confusion is often fueled by stereotypic expectations of **others**. When **others** play roles that challenge or defy stereotypic assumptions about older employees, people of color, women, and so on, they are often resented or regarded as exceptions to the prevailing rule. For example, an older employee who is eager to be promoted might be considered exceptional if the prevailing stereotype in the workplace assumes that people over 50 have no career aspirations. A woman who refuses to serve as note taker in a meeting might be considered "uppity" if her co-workers assume that the task is gender-related and appropriate for women only.

Exclusion/Isolation/Cultural Separatism

Because most employees have little awareness of how to communicate or interact effectively with **others**, many avoid contact with those of different core identities. In mixed work groups—where mainstream and diverse employees work together—it is not uncommon for people to informally group themselves by age, occupational level, gender, and race during coffee breaks and over lunch, thereby avoiding informal contact with **others**. This lack of informal interaction often leads to strained, artificial work relationships when prolonged contact occurs on the job.

While the consequences of cultural separatism can be detrimental for everyone in the workplace, the impact on **others** can be particularly negative. Lack of informal contact with members of the dominant group can lead to exclusion from key committees and decision-making groups, as well as social isolation at higher levels of the organization—where diversity is particularly limited.

Victims of Stereotypes and False Assumptions

Because increased contact and awareness are required to dispel false assumptions about **otherness**, cultural separatism in the workplace tends to reinforce stereotypes and false assumptions. The less sustained contact there is among culturally diverse individuals, the less likely it will be that opinions about **otherness** will be based on experience and real facts rather than myths and inaccurate generalizations.

Because members of the dominant group have more organizational power than **others**, they are less likely to be victimized by negative assumptions made about them. In the case of diverse employees, however, negative stereotyping can have very serious and detrimental effects on their ability to succeed. Stereotypes reinforce the assumption that **otherness** is a deficiency and that those who differ from the dominant group are somehow inferior.

Few Powerful Nontraditional Role Models

Considering the pressure to conform to the homogeneous ideal that exists within traditional organizations, it is not surprising that **others** have a difficult time finding role models to emulate. In looking up the career ladder, most diverse people see few successful senior managers who resemble them in fundamental ways. When it comes to the primary dimensions of diversity, role models tend to be rather limited. Where one finds an exception to the homogeneous rule, it is not unusual for the **other** to be in a high-level staff or support role with a smaller reporting organization, smaller scope of responsibility, and limited budget. It is also likely that this person will be under intense pressure **not** to interact with **others** of the same or similar core identity. The price of success for such individuals often includes isolation from the core identity group as a demonstration of loyalty to the mainstream organization.

Otherness as an Ongoing Source of Tension

While **others** may enter the workplace with optimism about their futures and commitment to their organizations, many lose their enthusiasm over time—as they recognize the importance of assimilating in order to succeed. In organizations where homogeneity is valued, diverse employees are reminded each day, in dozens of subtle and not-so-subtle ways, that they do not "belong." Because of the value placed on sameness, their **otherness** is seldom viewed as an asset and frequently viewed as a problem or liability by the organization.

As a consequence, **others** are often forced to struggle against the built-in bias that is an inherent part of every traditional organization's culture—at times resisting it and at times accommodating to it. Unlike mainstream employees, who can apply their energy to their work without overcoming major attitudinal barriers, **others** must often overcome the prejudices of peers, supervisors, subordinates, and the system—while maintaining enthusiasm and energy for their work as they do this. Needless to say, this is no easy task.

For many people of color and members of other diverse

groups, the added burden of having to manage these dynamics results in a condition called "mundane enviromental stress" (MES).[4] This means that by virtue of being different, **others** often experience a higher stress level in the workplace than their mainstream counterparts. A major source of workplace stress comes from the considerable amount of hazing that many diverse employees experience on the job.

Within most work groups, new employees are routinely subjected to a certain amount of teasing, joking, and ritual initiation by other group members. This hazing helps senior group members establish their dominance, test the new member's loyalty to the group, and ensure that unwritten practices or norms will be followed.

While the initiation of newcomers is commonplace and not limited to diverse employees, research has shown that the severity and duration of hazing increase as the dimensions of diversity of the new group member increase.[5] Therefore, a member diverse along the dimensions of age, gender, race, sexual/affectional orientation, and physical ability would be likely to experience more severe testing and hazing than would others who fit the mainstream profile more closely.

IMPACT OF ASSIMILATION ON THE DOMINANT GROUP

While homogeneity and assimilation exert a powerful impact on **others**, they also influence the perspectives of members of the dominant group. Although most dominant group members are unaware of the cultural context in which they work, their perspectives, opportunities, and judgments are nonetheless influenced by the value placed on homogeneity and assimilation. More important, their relative comfort and success operating within the traditional culture gives dominant group members a different view of the organization from the views of diverse employees. By and large, it is a more positive view, which minimizes the enormous impact of the corporate culture on various groups and, instead, focuses on the importance of individual effort.

The Rugged Individualist Myth

Within traditional organizations, most mainstream employees fail to recognize the power of the traditional culture in shaping opportunities and expectations. They do not recognize how their own success is linked to the norms, habits, biases, and traditions of the culture. They do not acknowledge that they derive benefit and support from it. Instead, they tend to view themselves as individuals *only* and regard their success as the direct result of their personal effort.

In most traditional organizations, it is not unusual to hear mainstream employees proclaim they "made it without any special help." The implication behind such statements is that diverse employees seem to require something "special" in the way of training and tangible support in order to succeed. What these statements fail to acknowledge is the important role that the organization culture plays in automatically supporting members of the mainstream—as it withholds support from **others**. Instead, there is a widespread belief among members of the dominant group that they have achieved success because of "individual effort," while the success of diverse employees is regarded as the result of "special help."

The Unqualified Rationale

While dominant group members tend to see themselves as high-achieving individuals, their view of **others** is usually quite different. Because diversity is not valued within traditional organizations, the advancement of women, people of color, and other diverse groups is often seen as a "bad compromise" made to "appease the government." As a result, when a diverse person is hired or promoted, mainstream employees will often express concern over the "lowering of performance standards" within the organization.

Since they do not consciously recognize homogeneity as a standard and assimilation as a norm, those in the dominant group do not appreciate that their criticisms of diverse employees are often a direct expression of this reality. They do not recognize that **it is otherness itself that is the central issue**. Yet, their criticisms frequently reflect the belief that being different inherently means one is less competent. Thus, the infusion of

others into the workplace is invariably seen as a lowering of performance standards.

Ongoing Reinforcement of Core Values

Within traditional organizations, there is a strong belief in the "rightness" of the dominant group's values—because these values are consistently reinforced within the culture. To the extent that one succeeds by emulating the homogeneous ideal or fails to succeed by not doing so, then the value of homogeneity and the need for assimilation become self-evident.

As such, mainstream employees do not need to be convinced of the value of homogeneity. Their accumulated experience and their success teach them that the traditional culture is viable and worth preserving. Since preserving the traditional culture means passing it on, most successful mainstream employees become strong advocates for the traditional culture—firm in the belief that they are helping **others** adapt and succeed as they proclaim its merits.

If there is any hesitation by members of the dominant group to preserve and defend the traditional culture, this reluctance is usually transparent to those on the outside. In an era of media coaching, sound bites, and "spin doctors," it is not surprising to find few organization leaders willing to speak openly and candidly about the difficulties and challenges their institutions face in a rapidly changing world. Instead of acknowledging the need for culture change to respond to new demands in the workplace and the marketplace, most senior managers talk about their organizations as though little or no change is required. Their reluctance to criticize the existing culture further reinforces assimilation as a valued institutional norm. It places the burden of change on **others** and affirms the false assumption that managing diversity requires nothing more than "doing business as usual."

In traditional organizations, we see countless examples of executives who vehemently deny that the traditional culture plays a part in promoting ageism, elitism, heterosexism, racism, sexism, and so on, through the value that is placed on homogeneity. Yet, the unconscious maintenance and reinforcement of a homogeneous culture does precisely that. It assures the continued underutilization of diverse human resources and blames diverse employees for their own lack of acceptance and success within the culture. Instead of blaming the victims, it is time for America's leaders to become outspoken critics of the organization cultures they represent—and proponents of change aimed at making U.S. organizations less exclusive and more inclusive, less divisive and more productive.

Cultural Myopia

Among members of the dominant group in any traditional organization, there is often a low level of awareness of multicultural issues and widespread inability to understand the impact of the traditional organization culture on **others**. It is as though group members suffer from a common disease that affects their powers of perception. We refer to this condition as **cultural myopia—the belief that one's particular culture is appropriate in all situations and relevant to all others.**

Cultural myopia tends to be more prevalent among those who are most comfortable in and committed to the traditional culture. The more connected an individual is to the dominant group's values, the greater the probability of cultural myopia. While cultural myopia makes it far more difficult for individuals to clearly see multicultural issues, this condition can be corrected. The first step is acknowledging the problem.

Once the problem of cultural myopia is recognized, managers can do much to reduce its negative impact. In particular, they can embark on an educational effort aimed at increasing their own awareness of:

- Barriers that assimilation creates as a strategy for managing employee diversity.

- Specific multicultural issues that exist within their organization.

- Impacts of these issues on diverse and mainstream employees.

In order to institutionalize the value of employee diversity and manage it as a vital resource, multicultural issues must first be viewed from a variety of perspectives: the individual perspective, the organizational perspective, and **the perspective of the other**. With the aid of increased awareness, it then becomes possible for individuals to accurately assess their own readiness to manage diversity effectively. Without this enhanced perspective, it is likely that most managers will continue to suffer from the effects of cultural myopia—treating everyone as if they were the same and measuring all diverse **others** by the same behavioral yardstick. Unfortunately, they will be applying a measurement that bears little relation to the realities of the contemporary American workplace.

NOTES

1. Ishmael Reed, "America: The Multi-National Society," *Multi-cultural Literacy* (St. Paul, Minn.: The Graywolf Press, 1988), p. 159.
2. *Korn/Ferry International's Executive Profile: A Survey of Corporate Leaders in the Eighties* (Los Angeles: Korn/Ferry International, 1986), p. 23.
3. *CEO* (Chicago: Heidrick and Struggles, 1987), p. 11.
4. Dani Monroe, "The Multi-Cultural Workplace: Its Challenges for the OD Profession," *Vision/Action*, December 1989, p. 8.
5. Natasha Josefowitz and Herman Gadon, "Hazing: Uncovering One of the Best-Kept Secrets of the Workplace," *Business Horizons*, May–June 1989, p. 22.

PART
II

Managing Key
Issues

Chapter Four

Beyond Stereotypes: Developing Authentic Relationships with Diverse Others

"I know that I am often not taken seriously in my work simply because of my Hispanic appearance. Before I say a word, I'm prejudged because I don't have a white complexion. It's not something that's talked about all the time, but it's always there. Every Hispanic thinks about it."[1]

Omar Alvarez, Mortgage Loan Agent

I magine a group of five executives in a Fortune 500 company meeting to discuss the feasibility of increasing the percentage of people of color and women on the board of directors from 10 percent to 50 percent. Given the nature of the proposed change, one would normally expect a vigorous debate to ensue. But this particular conversation is a role play in a corporate workshop on "valuing diversity." It is primarily designed

to point out the power of labels and stereotypes—not the benefits or costs of such a change in board membership.

To illustrate how stereotypes are often associated with primary and secondary dimensions of diversity, each participant
wears a headband with a particular identity written on it for
other group members to see. The five identities or labels include:

(1) Working Mother.

(2) Differently Abled Employee.

(3) Woman—Age 62.

(4) White Male Leader.

(5) Black Union Official.

STEREOTYPING DEFINED

As the role play discussion begins, the instructor tells all the
players to treat each other according to the stereotypes that are
often associated with the primary and secondary dimensions of
diversity represented by each label. She explains that a **stereotype is a fixed and distorted generalization made about all
members of a particular group.** She states that stereotypes ignore individual differences. They are rigid judgments made
about **others** that do not take into account the here-and-now
specifics of the person or the situation.

She goes on to emphasize that all groups share unique characteristics that are not stereotypes. This is because differences
in core identity lead to real differences in values, attitudes, and
behavior. Sometimes these real differences can be oversim-
plified and distorted. In these situations, they become stereotypes used to negatively prejudge **others.**

While all five participants can see the identities that other
players have been assigned by reading their headbands, they
do not know their own identities and cannot see the headbands
they themselves are wearing. Instead, they must guess what
their assigned identities are based upon the way others relate
to them during the discussion.

The Labeling Exercise

As the role play begins, all eyes are upon the "white male leader." "What do *you* think we should do?" is the first question asked. As the "leader" responds, one group member asks a clarifying question. But because the "differently abled employee" has asked the question, it is ignored by the group. Visibly distressed by the group's reaction, the "differently abled employee" makes another attempt to contribute, but to no avail.

Noting that the discussion seems to be stalled, the "black union official" then offers a suggestion regarding how the group might proceed. Before he finishes speaking, a member scolds him for his "extremist" point of view. Attempting to redirect the focus of the discussion, the "older woman" jumps in and offers several ideas. Nothing she says is taken seriously by the group. Instead, her comments produce snickers and impatient sighs around the table. Finally, when she attempts to express a personal opinion, the "working mother" is rebuked by two other members who advise her to "get with the program or get back on the mommy track."

Without the benefit of scripts or coaching, most people know how to stereotype **others.** In this particular role play (which has been used in diversity workshops within many organizations), there is seldom confusion among the players regarding how to treat a "white male leader" or a "black union official." People know which stereotypes to apply. What's more, it seldom takes longer than five minutes for most group members to recognize which dimensions of diversity they are being "typed" to. Although they are instructed to be themselves and to act naturally during the role play, most participants begin to behave according to group-imposed stereotypes within the first few minutes of this discussion. As such, the "differently abled employee," "older woman," and "working mother" tend to withdraw and shut down, while the "black union official" often becomes more challenging and the "white male leader" takes greater control.

PREJUDICE VERSUS GENERALIZING

While generalizations are often helpful in processing information and making decisions, stereotypes are not. They are too narrow, rigid, and judgmental to be of much use. Unlike generalizations that are based upon knowledge and past experiences, stereotypes are distortions, inaccuracies, and exaggerations. They are specific assumptions that support an underlying prejudice or fundamental bias about **others.**

Although prejudging and generalizing are essential processing functions that help us manage our daily lives, **prejudices are judgments made about others that reinforce a superiority/ inferiority belief system.** Typically, a prejudice will exaggerate the value of a particular group while it diminishes the worth of **others.** Stereotypes are then used as more specific evidence to support and reinforce a fundamental prejudice.

As an example, let's consider the individual who believes that men are innately superior to women. When challenged by someone, this person might point to great male inventors, world leaders, educators, and philosophers as evidence of the superiority of men throughout history and to the relatively low status of women in the workplace and in national politics as evidence of their lack of ability. As further evidence of the alleged inferiority of women, the person might assert that women are "too emotional to be effective." Specific examples in which women leaders cried in public might then be used to reinforce this point.

Listening to this argument, one would conclude that this person is prejudiced in favor of men and against women. The underlying prejudice is fundamental. It prejudges one gender to be superior to the other. The specific stereotypes chosen by the individual, such as "too emotional to be effective," are used to "prove" or reinforce the fundamental prejudgment. In this way, stereotypes serve as testimony in support of the fundamental prejudice.

Unlike generalizing, which is grounded in logic, experience, and available facts, prejudices and stereotypes are rooted in false assumptions and faulty analysis. Fear and ignorance of the facts are often the basic causes.

When our false assumptions and stereotypic "evidence" are challenged by facts and logic, as rational beings we have the ability to make perceptual corrections. Yet, we sometimes refuse to give up our old, inaccurate beliefs about **others** despite compelling evidence to the contrary. Why? Because discarding old stereotypes requires rethinking the biased, superiority/inferiority belief system that they support. This belief system is cultivated and reinforced within us from early childhood.

PREJUDICE AND STEREOTYPING AS BY-PRODUCTS OF SOCIALIZATION

When we look back at patterns of early socialization, it is easy to identify the many sources of prejudice that children are exposed to growing up in society. Initially, we learn about the prejudices and stereotypes of our parents, teachers, and other authority figures in the educational, political, religious, and civic organizations we belong to. While we may independently reject some of what we hear as false, we accept much of what we are told as accurate, reliable information about **others.**

As we continue to grow, we expand our disinformation base and reinforce learned prejudices with the help of stereotypic media images. Role models in the popular culture also send us strong messages about appropriate roles for men, women, people of color, differently abled people, heterosexual and gay people, older and younger people. We also reinforce our prejudices with the continuous help of friends and colleagues.

Regardless of how hard we may try to remain objective, each of us develops some prejudices and stereotypes about **others** as a result of our early socialization. Since most of us grow up in homogeneous communities, accurate information about **others** is often extremely limited, while distortions and inaccuracies usually abound.

The result is that we grow up knowing very little about **otherness.** What we mistake for "knowing" is often nothing more than inaccurate judgments that we hear and accept as true. Relying on these distortions as "solid evidence," we develop and reinforce our personal views about the superiority and inferiority of **others.** Over time, as we seek out examples and situations that reinforce old biases and confirm our stereotypic views, this inaccurate belief system becomes stronger.

STEREOTYPING AND THE DIMENSIONS OF DIVERSITY

Nowhere is the tendency to stereotype greater than when human beings engage **others** of different core identities—without the experience and personal awareness required to distinguish myth from reality. If a person's core identity includes primary dimensions of diversity that are unfamiliar or unknown to us, we are likely to relate to this person based on the stereotypes that we associate with the individual's affectional orientation, age, ethnic heritage, gender, physical abilities/qualities, and/or race.

As human beings, we have all been socialized to regard some primary and secondary dimensions of **otherness** as inferior and to stereotype accordingly. While we don't all subscribe to the same stereotypes, we each subscribe to some. Within our multicultural society, where virtually no one is familiar and comfortable with all dimensions of diversity, stereotypes are commonplace. No group is invulnerable to them. Regardless of what our core identities may be, we are all considered to be **others** by some people. When they do not know or value us, they will often prejudge us according to the stereotypes they have heard.

Within the workplace, many stereotypes related to the primary dimensions of diversity are widely accepted by people of diverse backgrounds. Does their widespread acceptance mean these common stereotypes contain some kernel of truth? On the contrary. What they underscore is the enduring power of prejudices—and the role that socialization and mass communications play in maintaining and reinforcing these faulty judgments about **others.**

While each of us collects a unique set of stereotypes to reinforce our personal belief systems, some stereotypes are more likely to be mistaken for "knowing" than are others. These are the common distortions, false assumptions, and inaccuracies that are most often associated with a particular group that we encounter in virtually every community, corporation, government, and educational institution throughout the United States.

To appreciate how pervasive stereotyping is and how commonplace some stereotypes are, let us consider an incident that occurred recently when a diverse group of government employees gathered together for a one-day seminar entitled "Diversity at Work." At the midpoint in the workshop, the group of 20 participants was busy discussing the negative impact of stereotypes. Having reached agreement that everyone is socialized to be prejudiced and to stereotype **others,** the group was then charged with the task of developing lists of common stereotypes of which they were aware.

Posted around the room were dozens of sheets of easel paper with a single word written at the top of each sheet. The headings included primary dimensions of diversity such as:

Over age 50.

Under age 30.

Asian-American.

African-American.

European-American.

American Indian.

Puerto Rican.

Gay.

Lesbian.

Blind.

Deaf.

Man.

Woman.

Several headings also pertained to secondary dimensions of diversity, including:

Middle income.

Lower income.

Southerner.

Midwesterner.

Californian.

Vietnam veteran.

Roman Catholic.

Mormon.

Jew.

Muslim.

Union member.

Manager.

Secretary.

High school graduate.

M.B.A.

Ph.D.

As participants circulated around the room to read the various categories, they were given magic markers and asked to write one stereotype that they had heard under each heading. The facilitator told the group not to repeat stereotypes that others had already written and not to make anything up. Instead, they were encouraged to write down *all* the stereotypes they had heard about each of the groups listed.

In less than 10 minutes, the task was completed. Everyone had participated and every easel sheet listed approximately 10 stereotypes. In total, participants were able to identify more than 300 stereotypes about the various groups identified in the exercise. While this may seem extraordinary given the short time frame, it is not. In similar exercises conducted in corporations, government agencies, and universities throughout the United States, most people are able to draw on an extensive knowledge of stereotypes to complete this task.

At the conclusion of the exercise, group members were encouraged to revisit each list and to read all the stereotypes grouped under each heading. As they circulated around the room, conversation ceased. The harsh, succinct, limiting nature of the words written on the walls began to register with each person. When they returned to their seats, participants discussed their personal reactions. Several people described the experience as "depressing." Everyone in the group agreed that the stereotypes used to describe their own core identities were completely inaccurate. By describing their personal disappointment and anger regarding the ways in which they themselves were typed in the exercise, most participants came to appreciate the limiting nature of all stereotypes. Yet, there is no denying that these false, rigid assumptions are a large part of what people hear and believe they "know" about **others.**

To illustrate the telegraphic power of stereotypes, here is a sample of those commonly identified in this exercise by highly diverse groups. As you read through each brief list, consider how many of these stereotypic labels are familiar to you.

Age Stereotypes

Younger Employees:

- Wet behind the ears. Know nothing.
- No respect for traditions.
- Lack experience, therefore have no credibility.
- Not loyal.
- Can't be trusted with much responsibility.

Older Employees:

- Less motivated to work hard.
- Deadwood.
- Resist change. Can't learn new methods.
- Plateaued after 40. Buried after 50.
- "Fire" proof.

Ethnic and Racial Stereotypes

African-Americans:

- Good athletes and great lovers.
- Lazy.
- Militant and violent.
- Talk funny.
- Less intelligent.

American Indians:

- Dishonest.
- Drink too much.
- Noble savages.
- Oil tycoons and land barons.
- Squaws, bucks, and Tonto.

Asian-Americans and Asians:

- All have same cultural heritage.
- Xenophobes.
- Secretive and sneaky.
- Stoics.
- Taking over America.

European-Americans:

- White only—No ethnic heritage.
- Arrogant.
- Insensitive.
- The enemy of the oppressed.
- Can't be trusted.

Hispanics/Chicanos-Chicanas/Latinas-Latinos/Cubans/Puerto Ricans:

- Have same cultural heritage.
- Macho men and subservient women.

- Volatile and emotional.
- Lazy.
- Have big families.

Pacific Islanders:

- Primitive.
- Oversexed.
- Ignorant and happy.
- Childlike.
- Gullible.

Gender Stereotypes

Women:

- Catty and bitchy.
- Not serious about careers.
- Emotionally out of control.
- Sleep their way up the career ladder.
- Indecisive and less competent.

Men:

- Think they know everything.
- Macho.
- Suppress their feelings.
- Prefer subservient women.
- Nurturing men are wimps.

Physical Ability Stereotypes

Differently Abled:

- Physical impairment equals intellectual impairment.
- Charity cases. Fortunate to have jobs.

- Can't carry own load.
- Have no romantic/sexual/emotional life.
- Success is qualified. "Not bad for a handicapped person."

Physically Able-Bodied:

- Assume all disabilities can be seen and recognized.
- Patronizing.
- Deny own frailty/mortality.
- Amazed at accomplishments of differently abled.
- Overreact.

Sexual/Affectional Orientation Stereotypes

Heterosexual People:

- Insensitive.
- Homophobic.
- Uptight about own sexuality.
- "Less feminine" women are seen as dykes.
- "Less masculine" men are seen as queers.

Lesbians and Gay Men:

- Should not be parents.
- Sexual beings first and foremost.
- Sexually aggressive/hit on straights.
- Unclean and unholy.
- Choose not to be straight.

IMPACT OF STEREOTYPING ON OTHERS

Given the rigid, limiting, judgmental nature of these common stereotypes, what impact do such labels have on **others**? By negating people's individuality and value, stereotypes have a destructive, dysfunctional impact. In most situations, they minimize the talents, potential, and accomplishments of **others.** Even when stereotypes appear to be glorified exaggerations, such as "All Asians are mathematical whizzes," they set narrow, inflexible expectations.

When we view **others** in stereotypic ways, we tend to seek out examples that validate our faulty generalizations. To the extent that an individual displays one or more of the stereotypic traits ascribed to a particular group, then that individual's behavior is interpreted as being characteristic of the entire group. At the same time, the individual's full range of behavior is usually ignored or discounted.

For example, if we carry the prejudice that people of color are inferior to white people, we are likely to notice any incident in which a person of color makes a mistake or uses faulty judgment. However, when competence and sound decision-making are displayed by **others,** we will be far less likely to notice and may even ascribe the positive result to some other circumstance or to another white person.

Because each primary and secondary dimension of diversity is susceptible to stereotyping, individuals can be *simultaneously labeled* due to their age, ethnicity, gender, race, sexual/affectional orientation, physical ability/qualities, geographic location, income, marital status, military experience, educational background, work experience, and so on. As such, the number of stereotypes that can be ascribed to a single individual is almost limitless!

To the extent that people are different from ourselves and represent dimensions of diversity unknown to us, we are more likely to confuse stereotypes with facts, to label and to misjudge their **otherness.** This human tendency suggests that as diversity increases within the workplace, the potential to stereotype also increases. Because they distort reality, stereotypes inhibit the development of authentic relationships among diverse people. Instead of increasing the level of mutual respect and trust within a work group, stereotypes delimit the potential of those who are typed and forced to "fit" a particular label.

STEREOTYPING AS A SELF-FULFILLING PROPHECY

Beyond the personal anguish and interpersonal conflict that stereotyping causes when it occurs is the more damaging long-term impact. Left unchecked, stereotyping can play a major role in lowering creativity, productivity, and employee morale within a work group. It can even become a predictor of behavior. By continuously reacting to and reinforcing particular responses in **others,** we can increase the likelihood that these behaviors will prevail. If we "see" people as "incompetent" and treat them accordingly, they will act incompetently. If we relate to them as "exceptionally competent," they will behave in ways that live up to our expectations. When it comes to stereotyping the behavior of **others,** what we choose to "see" is often what we end up getting.

In order to reinforce underlying prejudices, we must continually seek out stereotypic examples that confirm our biases as we ignore or rationalize examples that do not. Occasionally, we may choose to make some individual an "exception" to the stereotypic rule. But as our biased belief systems continue to solidify, we allow for fewer exceptions in our dealings with **others.** Eventually, we view all individuals from a particular group as being the same.

PREJUDICE VERSUS DESTRUCTIVE "ISMS"

Assuming that we are all taught to be prejudiced and to believe some negative stereotypes about **others,** shouldn't the negative impact of prejudice be about the same on each of us? Aren't we all **others** in the eyes of most people? Furthermore, since there are more women than men in our society, shouldn't the bias factor disadvantage men more than women? In the states of California, Hawaii, and New Mexico, where people of color outnumber white people, shouldn't whites feel a proportionately greater negative impact from racial prejudices than do people of color? One would think so. Yet, most of us recognize that this is not the case.

The reason is simple. Prejudice alone is not responsible for large scale, social discrimination. If it was, we would probably share equally in its negative impact. Instead, it is prejudice and institutional power that, together, create social discrimination—the combination of a personal superiority/inferiority belief system and the power to impose that system on **others.** Without institutional power, we all have about the same ability to inflict pain on **others** with our prejudices. With the help of institutional power, personal prejudices can become something larger, more powerful, and far more destructive. When we use institutional power to reinforce biased belief systems and to disadvantage **others,** we transform prejudice into the **destructive "isms": ageism, colorism, ethnocentrism, heterosexism, racism, and/or sexism.**

For example, to be racially prejudiced, we need only be born human. To practice racism, we must use institutional power to impose our racial prejudices on **others** and, thereby, limit their opportunities. It is the systematic use of power to disadvantage and delimit **others** that separates the destructive isms from prejudices based on age, skin color, ethnicity, sexual/affectional orientation, race, gender—or other dimensions of diversity.

If we were to inventory all personal prejudices against **others,** we would likely find a broad distribution across all diverse groups. However, when we examine access to institutional power in our society, the distribution changes dramatically. One cannot help but notice that some groups are far more dominant than others.

Within the American workplace, the distribution of power mirrors society at large. To a great degree, the balance of power favors able-bodied people over differently abled people, men over women, European-Americans over other ethnic groups, white people over people of color, heterosexuals over gays, and those between the ages of 30 and 55 over younger and older employees. Consequently, it is the members of each of these more dominant groups who have the opportunity to impose their values and beliefs on **others** and to practice the destructive isms.

The first step in combating systematic social discrimination is understanding that it results from the combination of **prejudice**

plus institutional power. All of us can work to minimize the impact of personal prejudices. Prejudice is a universal problem that we can all strive to solve. But some of us are in positions to do much more to build mutual respect, cooperation, and trust among diverse employees. To the extent that we have organizational power as members of more dominant groups, we are in a stronger position to challenge and change institutional cultures. As such, we can modify or do away with institutional norms, habits, policies, practices, and traditions that perpetuate the isms. However, before we challenge our systems, we must first challenge ourselves.

MANAGING PERSONAL PREJUDICES AND STEREOTYPES

As previously discussed, stereotypes are used to reinforce fundamental prejudices and our personal superiority/inferiority beliefs about **others.** Over time, they lead to low trust, low productivity, and increased disrespect among people of diverse core identities.

To date, no organization has ever attempted to measure the degree to which stereotyping creates friction, wastes human resources, and distracts people from their work. Yet, to say that everyone has some daily exposure to the negative consequences of prejudice and stereotyping in the workplace is not an overstatement. While we may not be directly involved in each occurrence, we all witness countless examples where people misjudge **others,** ignore their potential or their contributions, and treat them according to type.

According to several recent university studies, stereotyping is a serious impediment to the career success of both women and people of color. In particular, these studies have shown that:

- Women leaders receive negative, nonverbal feedback when displaying behaviors positively reinforced in men.[2]

- People who display negative, nonverbal reactions to **others** are seemingly unaware that they are doing so.[3]

- Even when the performance of men and women was perceived to be equal, participants asked to give hypothetical pay raises consistently gave men more.[4]

- Counteracting negative impressions by becoming more assertive may not work well for **others.** In fact, the more women talked in one study, the more they were ignored.[5]

- The same principles of negative stereotyping have been found to apply to blacks as well as to women.[6]

Valuing diversity in the workplace means increasing awareness and learning to avoid stereotypes. It means recognizing the worth and dignity of **others** and treating people with respect. It also means working to diminish the negative impact of our own personal prejudices and stereotypes by following these five steps:

(1) Accepting responsibility for the problem.

(2) Identifying problem behaviors.

(3) Assessing the impact of our behavior on **others.**

(4) Modifying negative behavior.

(5) Obtaining feedback.

Once we *accept* our personal prejudices as an inevitable by-product of socialization, we can begin to look critically and honestly at the particular myths and preconceived ideas we were conditioned to believe about **others.** As we *identify* these inaccurate prejudgments, we also become more aware of the influences they have had on our past behavior. We see the actions we took to support or reinforce our own biases more clearly. Their impact on **others** also becomes more evident. Through honest dialogue with **others,** we learn more about the subtle impact of prejudices and stereotyping—the effects that are less visible but just as damaging. Once we understand the problem and *assess* its impact, we can begin to *modify* our behavior accordingly. Finally, after we have tried some new behaviors, we can *obtain feedback* from **others** about their impact. If additional modifications are required, we can then repeat this five-step process as necessary.

THE DISEASE MODEL FOR UNDERSTANDING PREJUDICE

Assuming we succeed at modifying our behavior, can we eventually be completely free of bias against **others?** Can we cure ourselves of prejudice in the same way we can cure a common cold or some other infection? The answer is no. Because prejudices develop slowly, over many years, they are resistant to instant cures. While we may quickly determine that a long-cherished stereotype is no longer accurate, our fundamental superiority/inferiority belief systems are much more difficult to modify and dismantle.

When it comes to heightening our awareness and changing our individual behavior, it is unrealistic to expect a "total cure" from prejudice. If we make this a personal goal, we are likely to become frustrated with our own progress. Therefore, viewing personal prejudice as a curable disease is an inappropriate metaphor. It sets us up for failure. It also makes us suspect in the eyes of **others,** who recognize the intractable nature of our bias. Instead of feeling reassured, aware people often shake their heads in disbelief when they hear a person proclaim, "I'm not prejudiced!" The statement itself is a sure sign of one's *lack* of awareness.

THE RECOVERY MODEL FOR MANAGING PREJUDICE

Instead of denying the depth and seriousness of the problem of prejudice, we can manage our own biases in a more productive manner. Each of us can learn to minimize the negative influences of prejudices through continuous discovery, reevaluation, and reprogramming—but this awareness development process requires ongoing attention. As such, we must view the future as a prolonged period of discovery *and* recovery.

As our personal awareness of **otherness** increases, we can look deeper and more objectively at old stereotypes, beliefs, and values. While we cannot rid ourselves of all personal prejudices, we can learn to manage them more productively—so they interfere less with our here-and-now perceptions and expectations of **others.**

The importance of self-management of prejudice was underscored recently in a major university study. In a series of experiments involving hundreds of participants, researchers found that while all participants were aware of negative racial stereotypes, "low prejudice" subjects were able to censor these inappropriate and negative stereotypes, while participants deemed "highly prejudiced" were strongly influenced by them.[7]

As opposed to achieving a total cure, we can learn to **censor stereotypes and prejudices** as we increase our personal involvement with **others.** We can also help institutions change by pointing out the ways in which the organizational culture and its systems can disadvantage **others** and impede their ability to contribute fully.

RECOGNIZING VERSUS JUDGING OTHERS

Instead of inaccurately prejudging **others,** we can develop greater awareness of **otherness.** This requires paying closer attention to differences and similarities that exist among diverse groups. While we are all individuals, we are also members of many groups based on differences in our core identities. Recognizing the influences of core identity on the values, attitudes, and behaviors of **others** can help us anticipate how they are likely to see and respond to situations. While such generalizations will not always apply, they will help us appreciate and respect **otherness** in many situations.

In the past, it was often regarded as impolite to call attention to core differences. As a result, people pretended not to notice the ways in which personal style, communications patterns, approaches to managing conflict, social etiquette, and so on differed among diverse groups. Even today, in some organizations, "valuing diversity" is viewed simplistically as "respect for the individual." As such, cultural distinctions between groups are ignored and calling attention to these differences is thought to be stereotyping.

For example, in order to avoid being labeled sexists, some male managers in organizations that see diversity as "respect for the individual" pretend not to notice the different conflict-management style used by many of their women colleagues. Although they perceive this nontraditional style to be highly effective, they are still reluctant to identify it as a real difference. In effect, they are ignoring **otherness** in order to avoid accusations of stereotyping.

But recognizing **otherness** is not the same as making negative prejudgments about it. Whereas prejudices discount and delimit **others,** acknowledgment supports and reinforces the legitimacy and value of real differences. Ultimately, such recognition can help us develop greater authenticity in our relationships with **others** and greater respect for differences.

IN SEARCH OF AUTHENTICITY: WHAT DIVERSE EMPLOYEES WANT

Regardless of what one's core identity may be, no one enjoys being type cast. Instead of being forced into a limiting role, people of all diverse backgrounds want the freedom and support required to be themselves. In addition, most people want more authentic, honest, and respectful relationships with **others** than they presently have.

One important step in developing greater authenticity is understanding what **others** want from their relationships with us. What would increase the level of comfort and decrease the tension between people of diverse backgrounds when they interact? Here are some of the common answers we have heard from diverse groups in dozens of awareness workshops and in interviews conducted for this book:

Younger and Older Employees Want:

• More respect for their life experiences.

• To be taken seriously.

• To be challenged by their organizations—not patronized.

Women Want:

• Recognition as equal partners.

• Active support of male colleagues.

• Organizations to proactively address work and family issues.

Men Want:

- The same freedom to grow/feel that women have.
- To be perceived as allies, not as the enemy.
- To bridge the gap between dealing with women at home and at work.

People of Color Want:

- To be valued as unique individuals, as members of enthnically diverse groups, as people of different races, and as equal contributors.
- To establish more open, honest working relationships with people of other races and ethnic groups.
- The active support of white people in fighting racism and colorism.

White People Want:

- To have their ethnicity acknowledged.
- To reduce discomfort, confusion, and dishonesty in dealing with people of color.
- To build relationships with people of color based on common goals, concerns, and mutual respect for differences.

Differently Abled People Want:

- Greater acknowledgment of and focus on abilities, not just on disabilities.
- To be challenged by colleagues and organizations to be the best.
- To be included, not isolated.

Physically Able-Bodied People Want:

- To develop more ease in dealing with differently abled people.
- To appreciate abilities—in addition to understanding disabilities.

- To give honest feedback and appropriate support—
without being patronizing or overprotective.

Gay Men and Lesbians Want:

- Recognition as whole human beings—not only as
sexual beings.
- Equal employment protection—like all other groups
have.
- Increased awareness among straight people regarding
the impact of heterosexism in the workplace.

Heterosexuals Want:

- Increased awareness of lesbian and gay issues.
- A better understanding of the legal consequences of
being gay in America.
- More dialogue about heterosexist issues with lesbians
and gay men.

As we move towards greater authenticity, we can increase our personal clarity and comfort managing diverse relationships. Our interactions with **others** can become more respectful and candid, as opposed to remaining tense and superficial. Ultimately, we can come to appreciate why valuing diversity is not only good for **others**—it is also good for us.

The first step is distinguishing between myth and reality—between stereotypes and facts. Viewing diversity as "respect for individuals" is not enough. In order to respect individuals, we must first become comfortable with their **otherness** by learning more about their values, perceptions, and cultural heritages. We cannot take this important step in isolation. Instead, we must interact with **others** to become more aware. Then, after seeing the world as **others** see it, we will know what we must do to be part of the long-term solution and not part of the problem.

NOTES

1. Frank Viviano, "Poll Shows Ethnic Groups Torn by Bias, Cultural Ties,"
   San Francisco Chronicle, March 27, 1990, p. 1.

2. Melissa A. Berman, "Talking through the Glass Walls," *Across The Board*, July–August 1988, p. 26.

3. Alison Bass, "The Bias below the Surface," *The Washington Post*, March 20, 1990, p. F5.

4. Veronica F. Nieva and Barbara A. Gutek, "Sex Effects on Evaluation," *Academy of Management Review* 5, no. 2 (1980), pp. 267–76.

5. Berman, "Talking through Glass Walls," p. 26.

6. Ibid.

7. Ibid.

Chapter Five
Decoding Garbled Communication

"If it's not worth the trouble to you to find out what I want to be called, then don't bother to call me at all. If you are going to call me Will when my name is James, you might as well call me dog or dirt or any other thing I am not."

Mabel Lincoln, Older Black American[1]

R ecently, the top 150 people in a large government organization attended a two-day management conference to discuss human resources issues. An annual event, the meeting is considered to be the most important one held within the agency. Planning usually begins six months in advance, with several staff assigned full-time to handle site arrangements, speaker selection, and scheduling. To assure quality control, all speakers invited to present are routinely asked to submit a presentation outline for prescreening by the conference committee. Slides and audiovisuals are also reviewed. Prior to the opening of the conference, a rehearsal is staged for every speaker. In short, nothing is left to chance. Every conceivable problem is anticipated. Every detail that can be managed, *is* managed.

Despite these laborious preparations, the conference committee encountered a major snag this year. During the opening session, several people in the audience walked out in silent protest over comments made by the conference keynote speaker. It seemed his continuous use of "you guys" offended some members of the mixed-sex audience. In addition, the protesters cited his repeated use of sports and military analogies as "inappropriate." They said he should have used quotes from more diverse sources and not limited himself to Lee Iococca, George Patton, and Donald Trump. Finally, they mentioned several of the speaker's joking remarks about senility and old age—stating that they were stereotypic and insulting.

As they discussed this feedback over lunch, several committee members seemed shocked and confused. Finally, one said, "We heard the same talk that they heard. In fact, we heard it twice. Yet, none of us found it to be offensive. Did we miss something?"

The answer to this question is an emphatic yes! What the committee missed were the ways in which the speaker's examples, references, analogies, and jokes devalued others. What also took members by surprise were the negative reactions from some people in the audience. As one committee member stated, "This incident never would have occurred a few years ago! Back then, no one would have noticed or cared if these things were said."

Today, more and more employees are noticing when jokes, innuendoes, metaphors, and everyday language demean **otherness.** Because of this growing awareness of the powerful role that language can play in reinforcing stereotypes, effective communication in diverse organizations requires more sensitivity and skill than ever before. It also requires knowledge of diverse styles of communication and an understanding of how stylistic differences can be put to effective use within organizations.

While many regard communication as a basic, straightforward management tool, it is actually one of the most complex aspects of managing a diverse workforce. Without awareness of nuances in language and differences in style, the potential for garbled communication is enormous when interacting with **others.** Therefore, to become effective communicators, managers and employees must increase their:

- Language sensitivity—knowledge of words and expressions that are appropriate and inappropriate in communicating with diverse groups.

- Awareness of stylistic elements of communication— knowledge of the key elements of communication style and how they and **others** use these elements to communicate.

LANGUAGE SENSITIVITY

While we may not always be aware of it, our ability to clearly communicate and our credibility with **others** are closely linked to language usage. To communicate effectively, we must have the knowledge required to anticipate how our message will be translated and interpreted by **others.** If we are unaware of nuances and innuendoes contained in our everyday language, then we will be more likely to garble communication.

When it comes to everyday language usage, the words we choose often tell people more about our values, attitudes, and socialization than we intend to reveal. Once said, we can be confident that **others** will react to the subtleties conveyed and interpret the implied messages behind our words. Therefore, the first step towards more effective communication is to understand how language reinforces stereotypes and to adjust our usage accordingly.

Guidelines for Appropriate Language Usage

While we can never predict how every person will react to what we say, we can minimize the possibility of garbled communication by following some basic guidelines for effective language usage. These guidelines include:

- Use language that is inclusive rather than exclusionary; for example, women, people of color, folks.

- Honor the preferences of **others** when choosing terms of address; for example, Ms. versus Miss or Mrs.

- Avoid adjectives that spotlight **others** and imply they are exceptions; for example, black doctor, woman pilot, older supervisor, blind executive.

- Use quotes and references from diverse sources.

- Avoid joking remarks directed at primary and secondary dimensions of diversity.

- Use metaphors and analogies that reflect diversity; for example, from the sciences, arts, and human relations areas as well as from the military and competitive team sports.

- Avoid terms that define, demean, or devalue **others;** for example, crippled, militant, girl, boy.

- Increase awareness of the genealogy of words viewed as inappropriate by **others;** for example, minority, handicapped, homosexual.

STANDARDS FOR APPROPRIATE AND INAPPROPRIATE LANGUAGE

Whether a word is appropriate or not depends on the standards being used by the sender *and* the receiver of a message. If those standards are different, then reactions to the same term will also differ. When it comes to effective language, it is critical that we be aware of the standards of **others.** That way, we can avoid "loaded" terms that may seem neutral to us but highly judgmental to people of diverse core identities.

For example, while the term *minority* is often used to describe people of color, it is both inaccurate and inappropriate. Since there are far more people of color than white people, it is numerically incorrect. Because it implies less power as in "majority versus minority," it is also inappropriate in organizations that value and support diversity. Today, the expression "people of color" is increasingly accepted as the term of choice. Although often regarded as a new term, it was originally used in the early 1800s in French-speaking colonies to refer to **gens de couleur libèrès** or free people of color.[2] While it does not acknowledge the racial and ethnic diversity that exists within this highly diverse group, it does avoid implicit judgments about numerical or power advantage.

A term that is accepted by some but not all members of the group it describes is *Hispanic*. To many Latinas, Cubanos, Chicanos, and others more closely aligned with their Latin American and Indian roots than with their Spanish heritage, the term is less appropriate. It places more emphasis on European lineage and less on Latin American ethnicity. Yet, to others of the same ethnic background, *Hispanic* is synonymous with Chicano, Mexican-American, Latina, Cubano, Puerto Rican, and so on. As one Mexican-American writer put it, "To be Hispanic is to be part of the universality of being Latin."[3]

In some cases, words that are widely accepted by **others** may *still* warrant revaluation because of the subtle messages that they convey. For example, although commonly used to refer to both men and women, *guys* is a reference that ignores women. At a subtle level, it reinforces assimilation by implying that it is appropriate for a woman to be included as "one of the guys." While the generic use of *guys* may seem like a trivial issue to some women as well as some men, the word is inappropriate and out of synch with the philosophy of acknowledging and valuing diversity.

Lady is another term that many consider inappropriate in view of the expanding roles and responsibilities of most women today. The term was used historically to describe women of gentility and mannerly deportment who often relied on the protection of men to survive. By implication, a lady wore white gloves, was fragile, helpless, and always polite. Today, *lady* fails to take into account women's independence and equal status in society. As such, the word which describes an adult female, *woman*, is the reference least likely to create a negative response and most likely to be seen as descriptive rather than restrictive by **others.**

As our language evolves to reflect and respect the diversity within our society, some words in common use are becoming less acceptable as their origins are better understood. If we examine the genealogy of these words, we often find that they were originally coined to diminish, restrict, or negatively define **others.** For example, the term *homosexual* was historically used within the medical community to describe a serious psychological disorder. While this is no longer the case, *homosexual* continues to define gay men and lesbians as sexual beings only. Like *male* and *female*, the term does not take into account the complexity or totality of the person. Therefore, the use of *gay* and *lesbian* is considered to be more descriptive, more encompassing, and nonjudgmental.

The term *handicapped* is another commonly used term with a negative genealogy. Historically, the word was used in England to refer to the "extra weight or other conditions imposed in equalizing chances; hence, any encumbrance or disability that weighs upon effort."[4] This implicit notion of added weight is still associated with the term today—when it is used to refer to differently abled individuals. While *physically disabled* is a more descriptive and less loaded term, it is also one that focuses on the problem and not on the total person. Because it acknowledges physical and/or developmental differences while focusing on abilities, the term *differently abled* is becoming more accepted today.

Lexicon of Appropriate Terms

While there is no complete or comprehensive list of "correct" words to use in communicating with **others,** the lexicon of appropriate language is becoming more clearly defined. In an effort to increase respect for **others** and decrease the frequency of garbled communications, here is a brief list of terms considered to be more and less appropriate in communications with **others.** This list does not include perjorative terms that are consciously used to demean **others** (e.g., obvious racial or ethnic slurs). Rather, the inappropriate terms listed here include some which people use to convey respect for **others.** Nonetheless, they can sometimes elicit a negative response.

When Referring to	Use	Instead of
Women	Women	Girls, ladies, gals, females
Black people	African-Americans, Caribbean-Americans. Black people, people of color	Negroes, minorities

When Referring to	Use	Instead of
Asian people	Asian-Americans, Japanese, Koreans, Pakistanis, etc. Differentiate between foreign nationals and American born. People of color	Minorities
Pacific Islanders	Pacific Islanders, Polynesians, Maoris, etc. Use island name, e.g., Cook Islanders, Hawaiians. People of color	Asians, minorities
American Indians	American Indians, Native Americans, Name of tribe, e.g., Navajo, Iroquois. People of color	Minorities
People of Hispano–Latin-American origin	Latinas/Latinos, Chicanas/Chicanos. Use country of national origin, e.g., Cubanos, Puerto Ricans, Chileans. People of color, Hispanics	Minorities, Spanish-surnamed
Gay men and lesbians	Gay men, lesbians	Homosexuals
Differently abled people	Differently abled, developmentally disabled, physically disabled, physically challenged	Handicapped, crippled
White people	European-Americans. Use country of national origin, e.g., Irish-Americans, Polish-Americans. White people	Anglos, WASPS
Older/younger adults	Older adults, elderly, younger people, young adults	Geriatrics, kids, yuppies

ACKNOWLEDGING DIVERSE STYLES OF COMMUNICATION

The use of appropriate language can do much to improve the quality and effectiveness of our communications. However, stylistic variables must also be taken into account if we are to accurately interpret the messages of **others.** Because of sociocultural differences, people often employ different methods and styles of communication to convey the same message. This occurs even when they are using the exact same language. If we fail to appreciate how styles differ, we are likely to evaluate **others** through the lens of our own socialization. When we see behavior that varies from our own, we may find it confusing or judge it as ineffective. Until we recognize subtle differences in the communication styles of **others,** we will expect them to behave exactly as we do. Consequently, our communications will be garbled as we continuously misread and misinterpret their actions.

Today, as cultural diversity increases in the workplace, many managers and employees are searching for a comprehensive set of rules to follow when communicating with **others.** If one were to compile a list, the "do's and don'ts" of effective cross-cultural communication would probably fill several volumes—and still not prepare us for every situation.

Rather than focus on rules, we can improve the quality of our communications with **others** by learning to recognize key variables in communication style. By becoming aware of the specific elements of our own styles and how we interact, we can more accurately gauge the impact of our style on **others.** Similarly, by noticing the subtle differences in the way **others** communicate, we can reduce the likelihood that we will misinterpret or be confused by their behavior when it does not mirror our own.

ELEMENTS OF COMMUNICATION STYLE

There are eleven key elements of personal communication style. Each element is linked to sociocultural conditioning and the primary and secondary dimensions of diversity. These stylistic elements are often responsible for garbled communications that occur between members of diverse groups. In particular, the elements of communication style include:

(1) Mode of interaction.

(2) Reference point.

(3) Authority base.

(4) Degree of self-disclosure.

(5) Mode of expression.

(6) Method of support.

(7) Method of disagreement.

(8) Vocal characteristics.

(9) Method of assertion.

(10) Physical proximity.

(11) Reliance on protocol.

Regardless of differences in core identity, everyone's personal communication style is composed of these eleven basic elements. However, based on our core identities, we learn to employ each element in a particular way. The way we express each element varies among individuals. Our individual style of expression is linked to cultural programming and the primary dimensions of diversity—particularly ethnicity, gender, and race. This personal style reflects our values and beliefs about appropriate and inappropriate behavior. It is an approach to communication established early in life—based largely on the way family members talked to us and expected us to respond.

Each element of communication style can best be understood as a behavioral continuum that includes a range of responses. The end points on this continuum represent behavioral polarities. Depending on our socialization and core identity, our personal style falls somewhere on this continuum. The particular point represents our preferred or "typical" style of interaction.

Listed below are the behavioral polarities contained in each of the elements of personal communication style. As you examine each continuum, try to determine where you would place yourself based on your day-to-day interactions. Pay particular attention to any element where you are close to one end of the continuum.

Mode of Interaction:

Initiating ---------------------- **versus** ---------------------- **Listening**

The degree to which one initiates discussion or listens and responds as a *primary* mode of interaction.

Reference Point:

Individual -------------------- versus -------------------------- **Group**

The degree of emphasis placed on personal involvement and achievements versus group involvement and achievements in communications.

Authority Base:

Facts -------------------------- versus ---------------------- **Intuition**

The degree to which one relies on factual data versus intuitive judgments as the basis for reasoning and persuading.

Degree of Self-Disclosure:

Impersonal ------------------- versus ----------------------- **Personal**

The emphasis placed on tasks versus sharing personal data in building new relationships and communicating with **others**.

Mode of Expression:

Rational ---------------------- versus -------------------- **Emotional**

The degree of reliance on rational descriptions and facts only versus emotional reactions and embellishment.

Method of Support:

Challenge -------------------- versus ------------------- **Agreement**

The degree of challenge versus praise and agreement used to support others' ideas, views, and so on.

Method of Disagreement:

Confrontation --------------- versus ------------------ **Compliance**

The degree of confrontational versus compliant behavior exhibited in conflict situations.

Vocal Characteristics:

Low -------------------------- versus -------------------------- **High**

The vocal pitch, accent, and volume displayed in verbal communications.

Method of Assertion:

Direct ------------------------- versus ------------------------ **Indirect**

The degree of reliance on direct statements describing one's position or point of view versus indirect references, use of questions, and so on.

Physical Proximity:

Distant ----------------------- versus ------------------------- **Close**

The degree of physical distance versus closeness maintained and preferred in interactions with **others**.

Reliance on Protocol:

High ------------------------- versus ------------------------- **Low**

The degree of emphasis placed on formality and tradition versus spontaneous behavior in communications with **others**.

In examining each continuum, it is important to remember that no particular placement is considered ideal. Rather, every individual style can achieve positive results—when it is understood and valued by **others**. However, when stylistic differences are misinterpreted, garbled communication becomes the inevitable result.

The probability of garbled communication increases when we find ourselves interacting with **others** who fall at the other end of one or several behavioral continua and, therefore, use a different communication style. If we value behavior at each polarity, we will view both ends of a continuum as complementary. If we think of them as contrasting behaviors that are equally effective, then we will have less difficulty dealing with diverse styles. However, if we see some polarities as being in opposition to each other, we are likely to judge one polar behavior on the continuum to be more effective than the other. It is these judgments about the value and effectiveness of stylistic differences that often lead to garbled communications.

The greater the number of stylistic differences that we notice and do not value in communications with **others,** the greater the chance that we will misinterpret their intent or the message itself when we receive it.

PREFERRED STYLES OF COMMUNICATION

Based on our socialization and our past experience, each of us develops a preferred style of communication. The more successful we are using it, the more reliant we become on it. If we have limited exposure to **others**, we may assume that everyone operates in much the same way we do. However, when we move out of our familiar environment and begin communicating more with **others**, we often discover that this is not the case. If we appreciate the fact that stylistic differences exist and that they can be complementary, we can avoid making negative judgments and more readily accept the different behavior of **others**. However, if we believe that there is only one style that is effective—our own style—then we will often find communicating with **others** to be a frustrating and confusing experience.

Each element of communication style can pose a particular challenge when diverse people attempt to communicate. When we do not recognize or value the contrasting behaviors contained in each continuum, then unfamiliar actions and reactions displayed by **others** will be suspect. While the behavior of **others** may be as effective as our own, we will nonetheless judge it to be ineffective. To illustrate this point, let us consider how stylistic differences can contribute to garbled communication.

Initiating and Listening as Primary Modes of Interaction

In this instance, a discussion is taking place between colleagues who have different primary modes of interaction. The Initiator is a man who was socialized to believe that active involvement is a sign of intelligence, competitive spirit, and creativity. The Listener is a woman who was taught to see personal reflection as critical to understanding, analysis, and cooperative work relationships. Both place a strong positive value on their preferred modes of interaction. As such, they do not subscribe to the idea that initiating and listening behaviors are equally valuable forms of communication.

Given their assumptions, what will happen when they interact? The Initiator may conclude that the Listener isn't very

smart. He may think that she lacks creativity and is passive—
"a woman without ideas or ambition." At the same time, the
Listener may reach the same conclusion about the Initiator—
for different reasons. She may judge him to be reactive, superficial, and egotistical—"a man who likes to hear himself talk."
In each case, the value associated with a particular mode of
interaction prejudiced the person's reaction to the complementary style being used by the **other.**

Individual versus Group Reference Points

Now let's consider an American executive who is meeting with
a Japanese executive to discuss a possible joint venture. To impress his counterpart, the American begins by elaborating on
the success of his last merger. He talks about his business accomplishments at great length—always emphasizing what part
he personally played in the complex negotiations. To impress
the American, the Japanese businessman talks about how successful the company has been. He praises the efforts of the
work team in prior ventures and never describes his personal
role. Assuming the American's reference point is focused on
the individual and the Japanese's is the group, what might they
conclude about each other? If both men assumed that their personal point of reference was the only appropriate one, they
might react negatively to each other. The American might think
the Japanese was not forthcoming or had limited professional
experience in developing joint ventures. The Japanese might
see the American as arrogant and presumptuous—taking too
much credit for the work of others. However, if they understood this difference in their styles, they would be more likely
to have a favorable impression of each other.

Factual versus Intuitive Authority Base

One of the most notable differences in the communication
styles of many men and women is the preference for facts
versus intuitive judgments as a rationale for making decisions.
Because of differences in socialization, most men tend to rely
heavily on facts in arguing a point or making a decision,
whereas many women have been taught to "trust their intu-

itions" in sizing up people and situations and to use this information to "fill in the blanks." While studies have demonstrated that a combination of rational analysis and intuitive judgment often works best in analyzing complex problems and making decisions, many men still tend to discount the intuitive reactions of women co-workers as "unproven and unprofessional." At the same time, women often discount the opinions of male colleagues as "plodding, dense, and uninspired" when they rely on facts only to solve problems and make decisions.

In relationships where gender differences are understood and valued, attempts to force **others** to accept a different authority base become unnecessary. Instead, both women and men remain open to the influence of **others.** Together, they work to develop solutions and recommendations that reflect their varied perspectives and satisfy their collective concerns.

Degree of Self-Disclosure and Mode of Expression

In looking at elements of communication style, it is important to remember that ethnic groups that may appear similar also have different cultural histories. As a result, preferred styles of communication vary dramatically across ethnic cultures—even when race does not. An example of this stylistic diversity can be seen in the differences that permeate Western European cultures—particularly when comparing the elements of self-disclosure and emotional expression.

As a consequence of cultural influences, some European-Americans often garble communications when interacting with each **other.** Those who hail from cultures that emphasize reserve and emotional control may experience discomfort when interacting with **others** from more emotionally expressive cultures. For example, a Greek-American might begin a business discussion with talk about family and personal interests in order to break the ice. However, his British-American counterpart might want to get down to business immediately. As the discussion continued, there might also be differences in the degree of personal disclosure that each person displayed and expected from the **other.**

For people socialized to avoid personal references in business settings, the behavior of **others** socialized to share personal information and feelings can be a source of confusion. For example, a task-oriented person may have difficulty making sense out of a business meeting that begins with talk about family and hobbies. At the same time, those conditioned to make a personal connection *first* may be put off by the impersonality of **others**. They may interpret the avoidance of personal disclosure and emotion as signs of dishonesty. In each case, it is cultural myopia and ignorance of cultural differences that lead to garbled communications and negative judgments about **others**.

Method of Support

Next, let's consider a team meeting in which a white male account executive (AE) is presenting a new business proposal to a group of senior managers. Since this is a coveted opportunity to gain exposure to the executive tier, the AE has spent considerable time preparing.

At the end of the presentation, the AE invites the group to react to the new business proposition. The vice president of sales, a woman, opens the discussion by commenting on how thorough and convincing the presentation has been. She compliments the presenter and tells the group that she feels comfortable with the direction the project is taking. Listening to the feedback, the AE begins to feel confident that the proposal will be accepted.

Then the vice president of finance, a black man, enters the discussion. He begins with a challenging question about strategic intent. Then he asks a technical question about capital investment requirements. At this point, the VP states that he has some reservations about the overall proposal. He describes his reservations and asks the AE to respond to each one. Gone are the earlier feelings of confidence. Now the AE feels under attack.

Based on this round of questioning, the AE is convinced that the black VP will veto his proposal. Instead, at the end of discussion, the VP states that he is completely behind the new business proposition. He agrees to fund the project and the meeting adjourns.

Although pleased by the outcome, the account executive leaves the meeting still confused about the black VP's behavior. "I could have sworn he had it in for me because I'm white," he muses. "I'm really shocked that he liked my idea!"

What was the source of the garbled communication? While the AE recognized agreement from an **other** (the woman) to be a demonstration of support, he did not perceive that a challenge from an **other** could also be supportive. Instead, he experienced it as an attack.

The VP's challenge was actually an invitation to go deeper. It came out of a personal conviction that public debate is positive and that challenges test the validity of good ideas. While most of us can recognize agreement as support, in communications with **others**, we can easily misinterpret challenging behavior as a negative response even when it is intended to be supportive.

Method of Disagreement and Vocal Characteristics

To illustrate the potential for garbled communications in conflict situations, let's consider a white woman and black woman who work closely together. Based on differences in socialization, each woman has been conditioned to use a different style in conflict situations. The white woman, who sees herself as a peacemaker, has been taught to be conciliatory. As such, her behavior is characterized by attempts to smooth over differences. Speaking with a New England regional accent, the volume of her voice will often drop as the pitch increases. She will also exhibit more smiling behavior.

The black woman, who describes herself as a "feisty battler," uses a conflict style that is more animated and challenging. As such, her behavior is characterized by direct statements that emphasize areas of disagreement. Speaking with a Southern accent, the volume of her voice will usually increase as the pitch increases. She will also frown or display more emotion. Given their stylistic differences, how might these women perceive each other when they are engaged in conflict? Without some appreciation for the ways in which both styles work and the differences in their socialization, both women are likely to misinterpret the **other**. The white woman may think the black woman is hostile and recalcitrant. She may see her behavior as escalating rather than resolving conflict. Conversely, the black woman may think the white woman is weak and cowardly. She may interpret her behavior as an attempt to avoid conflict rather than resolve it productively.

As is true with all stylistic elements, the probability for garbled communication in conflict situations is greater when we are dealing with **others** who use a decidedly different approach from our own. When a person of like core identity uses a different style, we will often try to bridge the communication gap and attempt to understand the other person's position. For instance, in order to communicate effectively and avoid stereotypes, a white person from New York would have to adjust to the accent of a white person from Alabama, and vice versa. Would this adjustment process be more difficult or less likely to occur if the southerner was black? Quite possibly. When we are dealing with **others** of different core identities, our tendency is to go to stereotypes and judge behavior rather than understand and adjust to it.

Method of Assertion

Sometimes, we discover powerful differences in assertive behavior when comparing people of similar core identities. For example, while some women of color have been socialized to be direct and to express their desires and needs in a straightforward manner, many others have been conditioned to use questions and indirect comments to make their views known, to persuade **others,** and to argue their positions. When women of color engage each other in problem-solving situations without awareness of this important stylistic difference, they can garble communications and become angry and or disappointed with **others.**

For example, a Chicana who uses indirect behavior to assert herself, might interpret the directness of an African-American woman as overly aggressive. At the same time, she may experience a Japanese-American woman, who uses an approach *more* indirect than her own, as vague and overly passive.

Today, many women of color are eager to extend their support networks by focusing on commonalities and areas of mutual interest with each other. However, when stylistic differences are not taken into account within this enormously diverse group, they can become roadblocks to effective communication. Instead of increasing support among all women of color, these differences can lead to increased distrust and competition between ethnic and racial groups.

Physical Proximity

When it comes to physical proximity, each of us is raised with a definite idea about what constitutes "appropriate distance" for effective communication. While we may not be able to precisely identify the boundary, we know instantaneously when someone crosses it and encroaches upon our personal space. We also react differently when physical touch is used in communication and set personal limits that we expect will be honored.

But what happens when those limits differ dramatically? Often, less tactile people may wonder if **others** are being sexually aggressive. When they voice this concern, "How could you think that of me!" is often the response from the outraged **other.** Yet, there is no denying that touch is frequently used to signal sexual interest within our society.

Confusion and conflict over touch increase in the workplace when differences in role power are in evidence. For example, while it is acceptable for senior executives to touch subordinates in some organizations, the reverse is usually considered to be inappropriate. This is because touching is associated with the exercise of power in these organizations. As such, one can safely "touch down" but not "touch up."

As organizations come to recognize the value of employee diversity, they also become aware of the need to change old norms that diminish **others.** Frequently, one of the first norms to be challenged and changed is the use of touch as an expression of power. Regardless of sexual intent, it is usually considered to be both condescending and coercive by **others.**

To avoid garbled communication based on proximity and touch, it is important to be aware of the boundaries and tolerances of **others**. This often means that those with a high tolerance for touch and greater position power must modify their behavior. Once trust is established among people with different styles, it becomes easier for all parties to act appropriately as they use their preferred styles in communicating with **others**.

Reliance on Protocol

Let's now turn to another workplace situation in which we find two men—one younger gay man and one older heterosexual man—engaged in garbled communication. Both men are managers in the same organization and recently attended a two-week, off-site training session together.

While they were advised that "casual attire" would be in order during the conference, Bob, the straight man, chose to wear a jacket and tie to class each day. Bill, the gay man, wore jeans and sport shirts. Because he found the chairs uncomfortable, Bill chose to sit on the floor or stand during some of the class. Since the seminar was designed to be casual, he would sometimes make joking remarks and occasionally used earthy language to emphasize a point during class discussions.

While most group members liked his style, Bob was offended by Bill's behavior. He thought Bill was dressed inappropriately for a business meeting. He did not approve of his spontaneous humor or his earthy language. At the same time, Bill thought Bob was on "old, stuffed shirt."

Since that class, neither man will acknowledge the other at work. As a result of their earlier interactions, Bill is convinced that Bob is "an old, uptight homophobe." Bob thinks that Bill is "vulgar and immature." Based on limited interaction and quick assessments of each other, both men have now drawn important conclusions about the value of the **other**. While their assessments may be wrong, their intolerance for stylistic differences could preclude them from ever really knowing the **other** in more than a stereotypic way.

Stylistic Differences and Problem-Solving

When they are understood and valued, most stylistic differences can be accommodated within diverse work groups. In fact, when these polar differences are recognized and accepted, employees often agree that they can enhance teamwork and the quality of group interactions. Stylistic differences can make day-to-day operations more exciting and stimulating. Because they include a broad range of behavioral responses, diverse communication styles can often make routine problem-solving a more creative and productive process. However, when these stylistic elements are misinterpreted or devalued, they can lead to erroneous judgments about the competence, commitment, and candor of **others.**

HOW TO DECODE GARBLED COMMUNICATION

Because of limited exposure to **others,** most managers and employees lack the knowledge, skill, and experience required for effective communication. As a result, many find themselves feeling tense and confused when communicating with **others.** In some cases, they may try to avoid contact with **others** in order to reduce the level of tension. But as organizations continue to diversify, avoidance is becoming increasingly difficult. It is a strategy that postpones the inevitable—without solving the problem of garbled communication.

In order to improve the quality of interactions with **others,** managers and employees can take four proactive steps to decode garbled communications. They are:

(1) Identify personal communication style.

(2) Recognize personal filters and test assumptions.

(3) Acknowledge personal style in communications with **others.**

(4) Become aware of differences in cultural context.

Identify Personal Communication Style

Before we can appreciate the diverse style of **others,** we must become familiar with each element of our own personal communication styles. In examining the elements of style, it is useful to note where we fall on each behavioral continuum. How are we likely to act and interact? What positive values do we assign to certain behaviors? What behaviors, if any, do we avoid using?

Recognize Personal Filters and Test Assumptions

To the extent that we show a strong preference for a polar behavior, it is important to understand the value we assign to that polarity. It is also useful to consider what value we assign to the opposite polarity. How do we react to **others** who exhibit styles different from our own? What assumptions do we make about their competence based on the styles they display? Are we able to distinguish between style and substance?

Many managers and employees have difficulty distinguishing between the two. They will often judge the effectiveness of **others** on the basis of style—without examining results or outcomes. As such, the values they attribute to certain stylistic behaviors are like "filters" used to judge their appropriateness and inappropriateness.

Recognizing personal filters often requires feedback from **others**. Sometimes, this feedback may be difficult to accept. However, if we are committed to becoming effective communicators, then we will need assistance from **others** in order to identify our personal filters and blind spots. In assessing performance effectiveness, it is often useful to test and compare personal assumptions with **others**. When we find that **others** perceive the same behavior differently, we should ask ourselves if we are seeing a performance problem or reacting to our personal filters. In order to manage diversity as a vital resource, every manager must be able to distinguish between the two.

Acknowledge Personal Style in Communications with Others

Regardless of our core identities, everyone has a personal style that can be misinterpreted by **others**. To decrease the likelihood of this occurring, it is useful to identify those characteristics that **others** may perceive as threatening or confusing. For example, a black sales executive who works in a predominantly white office likes to challenge ideas as a way of understanding them. To reduce the potential for garbled communication, he often prefaces his comments by saying that he is a "deviant thinker." By informing **others** about his style, he believes he defuses stereotypes and makes communication easier for everyone. His technique allows the work group to more easily argue the merits of ideas without becoming personally defensive.

To the extent that we can inform **others** about our styles, they will often be less confused, less threatened, and less likely to garble our message because of stereotypes. While we cannot be responsible for managing the filters of **others,** by disclosing more about our personal styles, we can decrease the likelihood of garbled communication. The rest is up to them.

Become Aware of Differences in Cultural Context

Effective intercultural communication also requires knowledge of the varying importance of cultural context.[5] According to Edward T. Hall, a prominent intercultural theorist, differences in cultural context are often the root cause of garbled communication. In some cultures, context—the background and circumstances surrounding events—is extremely important in all communication. In others, it is often viewed as irrelevant.

Within relatively low-context cultures like the mainstream culture of the United States, messages are explicit—with the actual words carrying most of the meaning. Rules and regulations are also spelled out in great detail—leaving little for us to interpret. In high-context cultures, which include many Arab and Asian cultures, the words used to communicate carry only a small part of the total message. The rest is implicit in the context of the communication. As such, the communicator's standing in the community or organization, internalized norms that govern social behavior, and so on, all play an important part in high-context communications.

For many Americans, accustomed to operating in low-context environments, dealing with **others** from high-context cultures can be extremely frustrating. Because much is implied rather than explicitly stated in high-context cultures, Americans will often place greater weight on the words of an interaction than will **others,** missing the contextual message and misinterpreting the meaning. Without an appreciation for the important role that context plays, interacting with **others** from high-context cultures can be a highly confusing experience, at best. At worst, it can lead to many negative assumptions about the sincerity, intelligence, ethics, and so on of **others** and actually create new barriers to effective communication.

COMMUNICATING WITH OTHERS

In reviewing the points covered in this chapter, it is evident that communication becomes increasingly complex as diversity increases. With so many variables to be aware of, one might easily conclude that garbled communication is inevitable! However, by keeping three underlying principles for effective communication in mind, we can improve the probability that we will both understand and be understood more clearly in all interactions. These principles are:

- In all interactions, assume that you are communicating with **others.**

- Recognize that differences in primary and secondary dimensions of diversity will often produce differences in the way messages are sent and received.

- Above all, expect to be surprised, confused, and caught off-balance at times.

As we have seen from our discussion of language usage, the rules for effective cross-cultural communication are continuing to evolve. As a result, what is considered appropriate now may become less so in the future. To remain tuned in, managers and employees will need to heighten their awareness of stylistic differences and subtleties in language. They will also need to increase the frequency and candor of their communications with **others.** Only then can they hope to succeed at reducing the risk of garbled communication.

NOTES

1. John Langston Gwaltney, *DRYLONGSO* (New York: Random House, 1980), p. 67.
2. William Safire, "On Language: People of Color," *New York Times Magazine*, November 20, 1988, p. 18.
3. Rose Del Castillo Guilbault, "I Am Hispanic," *San Francisco Chronicle: This World*, March 5, 1989, p. 1.
4. William Little, H. Fowler, and Jessie Coulson, *The Shorter Oxford English Dictionary*, Vol. I (Oxford, England: The Clarendon Press, 1973), p. 921.
5. William B. Gudykunst and Young Yun Kim, *Communicating with Strangers* (New York: Random House, 1985), p. 12.

Chapter Six

Understanding Group Dynamics and Minimizing Collusion

"It's fine if you can get along with people. And, yes, we live in a society where some diplomacy makes good sense. But in the final analysis, you must not give up your beliefs in order to simply have people like you."[1]

Maxine Waters, California State Assembly Member

S o far in Part II of this book, we have examined the impact of stereotyping on individuals of diverse core identities. We've discussed language usage, elements of personal communication style, and reviewed the ways in which communications between diverse people can become garbled due to stylistic differences. If we were focusing only on individuals, our discussion of communication issues could now come to a close. However, increased diversity in the workplace does not just affect one-on-one relationships. Diversity has an impact on work teams as well.

To the extent that diversity is recognized and managed as an asset, it can exert a positive impact on productivity and cooperation within work groups. Because the philosophy of valuing divesity empowers all employees to put their skills and experiences to productive use, it offers organizations the potential for greater commitment and creative excellence. Conversely, when employee diversity is not managed as a vital resource, productivity and morale problems often result. Based on the value assigned to employee diversity, there is often a dramatic contrast in the performance of diverse work groups.

COMPARING DYNAMICS WITHIN DIVERSE WORK GROUPS

To illustrate, let us now examine dynamics occurring within two similar groups with diverse compositions. Group A is an organization that has institutionalized the value of diversity. Group B is an organization that states it values diversity but has not institutionalized it.

Within Group A, the general tone or climate is one of cooperation and mutual respect. Employees are encouraged to "be themselves" and to develop their own styles of communication. It it common for people of diverse core identities to help each other solve work-related problems. More experienced employees willingly assist their less experienced colleagues.

During team meetings, the views of all members are sought and considered. While there is usually spirited debate, most employees work hard to understand issues and resolve differences. They pride themselves on making timely decisions that reflect the best thinking of the group—not just that of a few members. Throughout the organization, leadership of team projects rotates, so that many members have opportunities to demonstrate their competence and build new skills.

Within Group A, most people feel free to challenge the ideas of **others** without fear of criticism or reprisal. Open discussion of productivity and morale issues is considered the norm. There are few attempts to hide issues. Instead, when conflicts arise, they are aired publicly and resolved after open debate occurs. While some group issues may be perceived as controversial, decisions rarely are. When they are announced by management, employees understand the reasoning behind them and believe they had an active role in shaping the outcomes.

Administrative decisions about vacations, lunch schedules, overtime, and so on are made taking into account the preferences of all employees. Group members often seek each other out off the job and many enjoy socializing together.

Within Group A, managers are viewed as facilitators of group effort and empowerers of individuals. While their diversity is valued, their core identities do not dominate. When employees need assistance, they do not hesitate to ask their managers for advice, believing that they are committed to helping all members increase their competence.

In contrast, the climate within Group B is characterized by competition and low trust. While employees often discuss the value of teamwork, most manage information as though it is a precious and limited commodity that cannot be shared. The importance of diversity is reflected in aggressive recruitment and hiring of people of color and women. Yet, when **others** join Group B, they are often isolated and left to "sink or swim" on their own. If a serious performance problem develops, corrective action is seen as the sole responsibility of the individual. If the person is unable to correct the problem, she or he is usually reassigned.

Within the unit there are many cliques—based largely on primary and secondary dimensions of diversity. These subgroups see themselves in opposition to each other—competing for limited opportunities and resources. As such, much energy is spent monitoring the access and opportunities of other cliques—to be certain that none is getting more than its "fair share."

The manager's primary role is that of rule enforcer and mediator. Because much time is spent resolving disputes over fair treatment, there is little time for coaching and developing employees. Due to the unconscious emphasis on homogeneity, there is no flextime and no provision for day care within the organization. However, there is a strict dress code and an absence control plan that managers are required to enforce without exception.

While the importance of team work and diversity are discussed monthly in staff meetings, they are not encouraged. Instead, subgroup members work together—united around the issue of inequity—with little commingling across their group boundaries. If employees step outside these cliques and begin forming collaborative ties to **others,** they are often pressured to give up external relationships out of "loyalty" to their sub-group.

At times, there is a lack of respect for **otherness** evidenced in the language and humor used within the group. Although many employees react negatively to put-downs directed at their core identities, they rarely object publicly. Instead, most use similar barbs to retaliate against **others.**

Generally, mainstream employees tend to be the most successful members of Group B—although they are not the numerical majority. While the unit has more than 100 employees, there are no known gay members. With few exceptions, most employees eat, interact, and socialize only with others in the same sub-group or clique.

DEFINING GROUP DYNAMICS

In order to understand the effectiveness of Group A and address the problems described in Group B, it is important to consider the group dynamics that are at work. By **group dynamics,** we refer to the **patterns of interaction that occur within groups that help or hinder the accomplishment of tasks.** Regardless of the clarity of goals and objectives, work groups can be highly productive or become dysfunctional because of subtle dynamics that affect individual and group performance. These dynamics pertain to the ways in which members interact with each other—irrespective of what the group's task may be.

To recognize these dynamics in action, one need only observe groups engaged in their work, taking note of:

- Who talks and listens to whom: how "airtime" is divided up, who is interrupted, who withdraws.

- Who is influential: whose ideas are utilized, whose are not, who is likely to agree or disagree with whom.

- How decisions are made within the group: majority-minority vote, consensus, compromise.

- How conflicts are managed within the group: win-lose, avoidance, win-win.

- How feedback is managed within the group: encouraged, stifled.

✓ NORMS THAT ENHANCE DYNAMICS IN DIVERSE WORK GROUPS

Many factors influence patterns of interaction within work groups—regardless of how diverse or homogeneous they may be. However, as diversity increases, four factors become particularly important for effective functioning. When these factors or norms are operative, they can enhance the quality of communication and interaction among group members and increase the likelihood of group success.

Unlike major policy decisions that require approval from the top before implementation, these norms can be instituted and supported by local managers and work teams. They require no policy changes, revised work practices, or other formal acts to initiate. Yet, when they are instituted, they can be more powerful than any corporate policy in fostering an organizational climate that values diversity. The four operating norms include:

- Open membership.

- Shared influence.

- Mutual respect.

- Candor.

While these norms are important within homogeneous work groups, they are even more critical as employee diversity increases. When they are used as guidelines for group interaction, they can decrease the likelihood of stereotyping and empower all employees to contribute fully. At the same time, these norms can help members manage new relationships and unfamiliar situations more effectively. They can reduce the initial tension many employees experience when interacting with **others** and help new members become full contributors.

Open Membership

Open membership refers to the extent to which individuals feel included, accepted without restriction, and fully able to participate in the work of the group. Within diverse groups that support open membership, new members enter with the same rights, privileges, access to information, and responsibilities as all others. Almost immediately, they are regarded by the rest of the group as "a part of" rather than "apart from." Their core identities are recognized and they are free to express themselves and to be themselves. They are included in group activities and encouraged to actively participate in important group events.

While new members are expected to contribute to the work of the group, they are also expected to go through a transition phase as they learn their roles, become familiar with the workings of the organization, and so on. During this period, members with more experience work to orient those with less experience to formal organization structures, informal relationships critical to accomplishing goals, organizational priorities, and specific tasks. When performance problems occur, new employees receive peer assistance that supports learning as it builds confidence.

The benefits of open membership continue after members become familiar with the work of the group. A spirit of cooperation and helpfulness permeates the unit and people continue to support each other, share information, and pitch in—without concern over who receives "credit" for the group's effort.

Shared Influence

Shared influence refers to the extent to which all group members affect goal setting, decision making, and the establishment of group priorities. Within diverse groups that encourage shared influence, the ideas and opinions of all members have weight. Key decisions that affect the members of the unit are not made without first soliciting group input. In such matters, it is considered a responsibility rather than a privilege to contribute one's thoughts and to share diverse perspectives.

Where influence is shared, it is not unusual to see some proposals altered significantly as their potential impact on all group members is analyzed and understood. Even after a decision is made, the manager and the group remain open to new input from employees at all levels. Throughout the work group, employees believe they can shape events and make a real difference. They believe this because many have actually done so. There is a history of collaboration and flexibility within the group that supports this belief. Unlike many groups, where the ideas of a select few are considered, diverse groups that promote shared influence do not restrict members' ability to participate because of primary or secondary dimensions of diversity. All ideas from all sources are assumed to have value.

Mutual Respect

Mutual respect refers to the degree of acceptance and support for **otherness** that exists among members of a work group. In diverse teams that encourage mutual respect, core differences are recognized and viewed as adding value to the group. Employees recognize the importance of understanding **others** and increasing their knowledge of multicultural issues. This need for expanded awareness is a shared goal among all group members.

In addition, group members are sensitive to the ways in which language and stereotypes diminish **others.** They are careful to avoid garbled communication and consciously monitor their own interactions in an effort to enhance the clarity of communication. The use of humor within the group also reflects the value placed on diversity. As such, jokes that demean **others** are regarded as inappropriate. When mutual respect is encouraged, there is no hierarchy of core identity issues. All primary and secondary dimensions of diversity are considered to be important and deserving of respect.

Candor

Candor refers to the ability of group members to raise issues, challenge **others,** and openly disclose personal opinions and feelings. Within diverse groups, candor is understood to be inextricably linked to mutual respect. As such, candor is considered to be beneficial and constructive when it enhances relationships and increases productivity within the group.

When candor is encouraged as an operating norm, serious issues can surface and be openly discussed. Critical information is shared with all employees. There is no "office grapevine" for political intrigue and gossip—because members know what is going on within the group. Employees recognize the difference between candor that respects **otherness** and candor that promotes divisiveness. Because their efforts are aimed at valuing diversity, group members are able to engage in productive conflict resolution without discounting or stereotyping **others.**

Most important, they understand that conflict is an inevitable part of group life. As such, they do not avoid it, rationalize it, or actively deny it when it is present within the group. Instead, members step towards the conflict and towards **others**—believing that, together, the group can resolve disputes more creatively and more effectively. In groups that value diversity, candor and mutual respect are the threads that run through the fabric of productive conflict resolution, performance evaluation, and all other processes requiring feedback and subjective analysis.

When diversity is valued within a group, managers and employees can do much to support this philosophy through their day-to-day interactions. In particular, they can promote this value by instituting and supporting the norms of open membership, shared influence, mutual respect, and candor. When all four norms are operative within diverse groups, interactions tend to be characterized by cooperation, inclusion, peer support, openness, creative excellence, shared recognition, and shared rewards. When these norms are not operative, a different set of dynamics is likely to occur, including competition, coalition formation, member isolation and harassment, active resistance, peer sabotage, and collusion.

COLLUSION

Of the many dynamics that can decrease commitment and productivity among members of diverse work groups, none is more pervasive or insidious than the dynamic of collusion.

Unlike active opposition to change, collusion is a more passive form of resistance. Therefore, it is often difficult to identify, isolate, and challenge. But while it may appear elusive at times, collusion is a powerful impediment to culture change. Within organizations that value homogeneity, collusion helps to preserve the status quo and to derail efforts aimed at culture change. We define **collusion** as **cooperating with others knowingly or unknowingly to reinforce stereotypic attitudes, prevailing values, behaviors, and/or norms.**[2] Although collusion usually restricts and delimits everyone's potential for growth and change, individuals repeatedly collude to protect themselves—often without being aware of it. It is self-protection that causes people to collude, as well as fear of rejection for speaking out.[3]

Origins of Collusion

To understand collusion, we must again go back and reexamine early patterns of socialization. For most children, being "well behaved" often means censoring thoughts, feelings, and actions. In effect, children are expected to conform to societal norms—even when they think, feel, and want to behave very differently from the way parents, teachers, and so on expect them to act. The origins of collusion are rooted in this socialization process and represent excessive accommodation and over-adaptation to one's environment.

As we grow out of childhood and become young adults, the social indoctrination process continues. We are encouraged to behave in ways that do not violate rules of social etiquette or challenge accepted practices and traditions. As we learn to accommodate to the social rules, we become skillful at colluding.

Over time, we learn that collusive behavior can help us adapt more successfully to new or threatening environments. We repeatedly discover that when we obey the rules, we are safe, and sometimes rewarded. When we resist, we are often punished. Because most of us want to avoid pain and increase our own comfort, we learn to adapt. This adaptation process causes us to rely on collusion as a protective strategy—one that we use frequently throughout our lives. The lesson learned each time we collude is: "You can avoid pain through adaptation."

Sometimes, the expectations of society challenge our personal values and beliefs. When this occurs, we face a difficult choice. Because we have learned that collusion is an effective survival strategy, we often choose it without thinking.

By the time we reach adulthood, most people learn to "live with" internal conflicts caused by societal expectations that are in opposition to personal values, preferences, and desires. In some cases, we may act in ways that challenge or undermine our stated values and then rationalize this inconsistency. The power of collusion and the protection it provides causes us to accept this paradox as "inevitable." In short, we learn to survive and gain acceptance through collusive behavior rather than risk punishment by being true to our convictions.

Collusion as a Survival Strategy

Very early in life, collusion becomes an important survival strategy for each of us. It is something we learn to do in order to manage day-to-day conflicts and gain approval from those around us. Regardless of core differences, everyone colludes at times. Every individual has the experience of withholding an idea or opinion because of fear of rejection or attack. To the extent that we do this as a routine, day-to-day practice, we may succeed in protecting ourselves. However, we also fail to disclose our true feelings and preferences. As such, we fail to inform others about our views or influence the course of events.

COLLUSION AND STEREOTYPING

Because collusion reinforces the status quo, it is often an effective method for maintaining stereotypes about **otherness.** When it comes to reinforcing stereotypes, collusion usually translates into the active or passive support of a biased point of view about **otherness.** Sometimes this support is preconscious—we are not even aware that we are giving it. Yet, even when it is not conscious, collusion can be a powerful obstacle to change. Within most work groups, we see three distinct types of collusive behavior:

- Silence.

- Denial.

- Active cooperation.

Silence

Of the three types of collusive behavior common in diverse groups, silence is the most prevalent. To silently collude, one need only stand back, observe inappropriate behavior, and do nothing to challenge or change it. Within groups where diversity is not valued, behavior that demeans or stereotypes **others** is often tolerated by group members. While the majority of the group may not actively participate in the harassment of **others,** they will ignore the negative behavior of those who do.

For example, members may remain silent when a racist joke is told or allow a negative remark about **otherness** to go unchallenged. By remaining silent at a moment when **others** are being victimized by stereotyping, members help to reinforce the status quo. In this way, they passively condone prejudicial behavior within the group and deny support to the victims of that behavior.

Recently, an American Indian woman working for a high tech company in Northern California cited collusion as one of the reasons behind her decision to resign after more than 10 years with the organization. She stated: "Last year, we launched a major diversity campaign in the company. There was training for all the managers and everyone was told they needed to become more sensitive to cultural differences. Because of my cultural heritage, I was already sensitized to the way ethnic jokes put people down. I didn't like them and I let people know it. But that didn't stop some of my peers from making inappropriate remarks.

"After my manager attended a high impact workshop, I had hopes that some things would change in the department. I thought he'd stop tolerating insensitive remarks and ethnic jokes in our team meetings. I thought he'd be out there more—calling people on their inappropriate behavior. But instead, he acted like he didn't see what was going on. If I confronted someone in the group, he'd stay out of the discussion and act like he wasn't a part of it. Frankly, I got tired of being the social conscience for the whole department. I felt like the diversity thing was just a lot of 'lip service.' There was no attempt to change the team's norms, which in my view, were racist, sexist, and homophobic."

Although silence can be interpreted to mean many things in group situations, the message to **others** is quite clear when members collude through silence. In such cases, silence is a sign of apathy, disinterest, and disengagement. It demonstrates a lack of respect, concern, and support for **others.** Without uttering a single word, silence can say a great deal about one's commitment to the value of diversity. When it is used as a form of collusion, it sends a powerful and disturbing message to **others** about their value within the group.

Denial

Unlike silence, which is a passive form of collusion, denial is more active. It is a method of colluding that attempts to negate the existence of a problem—despite compelling evidence to the contrary. Within many work groups that support assimilation, we find examples of **others** who learn to adapt and collude by denying. These are the individuals who insist that prejudice and the destructive "isms" are fictions. They repeatedly testify that, as **others,** they themselves have never experienced discrimination or observed it taking place.

For example, in a major national retailing organization, where women make up more than 70 percent of the total workforce but less than 5 percent of senior management, a group of women managers recently decided to establish a formal women's support group. The goal of this group is to improve cooperation and communication among all women in the company and to accelerate their career advancement into and within management.

As part of this effort to unify women at all levels of the organization, the solo woman officer of the company was invited to become a charter member of the new network. Much to the dismay of the other women involved, she adamantly refused to join in. Her refusal was based on a strongly-held belief that she "never thought of herself as a woman in business and, therefore, never let her gender get in the way." Not only would she not help the other women organize, her personal views challenged the basic need for a women's network by implying that the other women were letting their gender "get in the way."

Because their testimony reinforces the status quo and never challenges the organization culture, **others** who collude through denial are often rewarded for doing so. They become success models that the institution points to with pride. Yet, to **others** of the same core identity, these success models often appear to have been co-opted. They exhibit no understanding of organizational issues related to fairness and no empathy for **others** of the same or similar core identity. Instead of working on their behalf, they will often blame **others** for their own lack of progress.

Within work groups that are moving away from assimilation towards the philosophy of valuing diversity, denial can be a powerful form of resistance to change. Whether it is denial or discriminatory practices by **others** or the allegation of "reverse discrimination" by mainstream employees, this form of collusion shifts the group's focus away from finding productive solutions to a serious problem by denying the very existence of the problem. As such, collusion through denial is an effective way of stalling and derailing group effort aimed at change. By focusing attention away from the real problem, it adds an element of confusion to the problem-solving process and leaves some members wondering what the issues really are.

Active Cooperation

The third form of collusion found in many work groups is active cooperation among group members to reinforce stereotypes about **otherness** through personal actions. In such cases, we see individual members reinforcing stereotypes through their own behavior in an attempt to gain acceptance within the group. For example, in some groups, members may feel obliged to laugh at a joke that demeans **others** in order to be included. Sometimes we find individuals routinely playing stereotypic roles within a group in order to gain approval; for example, a woman always serving as note taker, getting coffee, or a man performing all the physical chores in an office—lifting boxes, repairing equipment. Making self-deprecating remarks and jokes about one's own core identity is another example of this type of collusive behavior.

When membership is conditional within a work group and **others** feel threatened by the attitudes and values of mainstream employees, it is not uncommon for some to camouflage their real feelings by colluding. Within organizations that support assimilation, collusion is a frequent response from **others** to inappropriate norms and rules imposed by the dominant group. While the work group and the organization may both assume they have the endorsement of **others,** collusion is not a demonstration of commitment to group norms or organizational policies. Instead, it is a self-protective response to a perceived threat and is often indicative of a serious morale problem within the organization. When **others** see collusion as their only means of acceptance and survival within the work group, the norms of open membership, shared influence, mutual respect, and candor are definitely not operative.

HOW TO BREAK COLLUSIVE BEHAVIORAL PATTERNS

Whether out of a fear of change, rejection, or punishment, most people find that there are personal, short-term benefits to colluding in some situations. Collusion often limits personal risk. It is an effective way of avoiding conflict. However, the destructive consequences of colluding with stereotypes and prejudice in the workplace are usually far more severe than the personal consequences of speaking out. Not only does collusion maintain deep divisions between people of diverse core identities, it also reinforces behavior and attitudes that reject diversity as a valued asset. To be "part of the solution—not the problem," employees and managers must learn to recognize the ways in which they collude and, thereby, reinforce negative stereotypes. Above all, they must be willing to break collusive patterns and speak out.

Generally, people wishing to minimize collusion in their work group relationships follow these three steps in addressing this problem:

- They seek assistance from other group members in identifying their own patterns of collusive behavior.

- Initially, they modify their behavior in relationships where there is maximum potential for success and minimal potential for irreparable damage—recognizing that it is often easier to try new behavior in low-risk situations.

- They introduce the formal concept of collusion and enlist the help of **others** in pointing out destructive dynamics operating within the work group.

Collusion is an aspect of individual behavior that needs careful self-examination—if one is committed to valuing diversity and managing it as a vital resource. Because we often do not realize when we are colluding, breaking out of collusive behavioral patterns requires feedback from those who see the consequences of our behavior more clearly than we do. Just as it is often easier to recognize prejudice in other people—it is also true that we notice collusive behavior in **others** more readily than we see it in ourselves.

Within organizations that value diversity, there is institutional support for individuals who refuse to collude and, thereby, perpetuate stereotypic thinking. Instead of being regarded as "malcontents" or "whistle blowers," these individuals are viewed as catalysts for productive change. Their willingness to speak out and challenge the status quo is regarded as healthy, not harmful. What's more, as they raise issues and educate co-workers about stereotyping and collusion, their numbers increase. Ultimately, breaking out of collusive behavior patterns that reinforce stereotypes becomes a shared responsibility within the work group. Both managers and employees see the benefit to themselves and others of abandoning coercion and collusion in favor of more open and respectful group interaction.

NOTES

1. Brian Lanker, *I Dream A World* (New York: Stewart, Tabori & Chang, 1989), p. 36.
2. Lee Butler, "The Anatomy of Collusive Behavior," *NTL Connections* 4, no. 1 (Alexandria, Va: NTL Institute, December 1987), p. 2.
3. Ibid.

Chapter Seven
Managing Culture Clash

"Pluralism requires tolerance. But a pluralistic society undermines its ability to deal with its most serious problems when differences are denied and tolerance is transformed into a false sense of unity. . . . A healthy pluralism may in fact be characterized by the mutual respect that arises from a simmering of conflicting viewpoints and diverse senses of identity."[1]

Elizabeth Kristol,
Executive Director—
Institute for International Health and Development

V irtually all major institutions in America—public, private, academic, and not for profit—have been built around the values, attitudes, and behaviors expressed in the homogeneous ideal. This ideal characterizes the dominant organization culture within the American workplace. Until recently, acceptance of the mainstream culture was rarely questioned aloud by employees. Instead, it was assumed that because leaders of most institutions exhibited qualities associated with this ideal, these qualities had to be important. Thus, most employees willingly adopted the homogeneous ideal as their ideal and became assimilated.

In order to assimilate, new entrants into the organization had to learn about the dominant culture. Such knowledge was needed to survive and succeed. However, members of the dominant group had no need to learn about the values, attitudes, and behaviors of **others**. They believed their way of doing things was the "right" way. Therefore, it was up to **others** to learn their methods and attempt to fit in.

Generally, the culture of organizations that valued homogeneity reflected a bias towards masculine experience and male-oriented behavior. As such, these institutions favored a competitive operating style, a hierarchical organization structure, a win/lose approach to conflict resolution, a rational problem-solving approach, an emphasis on analytical skills, and an aversion to intuition and the display of emotions.[2] Together, these elements formed a standard or model for managers and employees to follow. New employees recognized the importance ascribed to this managerial model. They understood that questioning the model could be interpreted as questioning deeply held organization values. Rather than put themselves at risk, they learned to adapt and embrace this model as their own. This adaptation process lead to many behavioral modifications by **others**. In particular:

- Women learned they had to strike a precise balance between being assertive and being feminine. If they failed to do this, they were likely to be perceived as too aggressive or too soft.

- Asian-Americans learned that being indirect was often perceived by the dominant group as being indecisive.

- African-Americans learned that displaying strong emotions in the workplace was dangerous to do because it often made white people feel uncomfortable.

- Lesbians and gay men learned that "coming out" could jeopardize their jobs and ruin their careers.

- Differently abled employees learned that requests for signing, wheelchair access, and so on were often viewed by the dominant group as "causing trouble."

- Latinos and Latinas learned that speaking Spanish on the job was often viewed by mainstream employees as conspiratorial.

By adapting to the dominant culture, **others** assumed they would survive and, eventually, succeed. Sometimes they did but often they did not. After decades of effort to fit the standard, many diverse people now recognize the futility of this effort. Today, more are choosing to organize and lobby for change. As they increase awareness of the need for change, they are building larger constituencies. They are helping more people recognize how stated and unstated policies and procedures can disadvantage **others** who cannot meet the test of the homogeneous ideal.

This increased awareness and political power has resulted in a myriad of change-related initiatives:

- Legal challenges to discriminatory policies and practices based on age, gender, race, and physical ability.

- Lobbying by differently abled groups to increase access to public buildings and public transportation.

- Creation of ethnic studies programs in most colleges and universities.

- Lobbying by gay and lesbian organizations for employment protection and legally sanctioned domestic partnerships.

As they occur, such intitatives often create confusion, frustration, and misunderstanding in organizations that do not recognize the needs of a diverse workforce. They have led to name-calling, walkouts, protests, boycotts, and have drained energy, commitment, and other resources within many organizations. In short, they have generated considerable "culture clash."

CULTURE CLASH DEFINED

Culture clash is conflict over basic values that occurs between groups of people with different core identities. Generally, culture clash occurs when the values, attitudes, and behaviors of the dominant group are questioned by **others** and, in turn, create a disturbance within the organization.

Today, as **others** grow more determined to preserve their unique cultural heritages and resist assimilation, culture clash is becoming more prevalent within organizations. Unlike the past, when these challenges were ignored by the mainstream, the political and economic resources of **others** are now causing organizations to respond differently. It is no accident that *Fortune, Time, Business Week,* and *The Wall Street Journal* continue to feature major stories about the organizational implications of an increasingly diverse workforce. Managing **others** and dealing with culture clash are becoming survival issues. For this reason, it is critical that managers in all institutions understand:

- Types of culture clash they can anticipate as **others** become the majority in the workplace.

- Predictable reactions that will occur when employees ask for change or are asked to change.

- Strategies that can be used to minimize the negative impact of culture clash.

TYPES OF CULTURE CLASH

There are three distinct types of culture clash. Each type describes the way in which the clash or challenge is perceived by the organization and by members of the dominant group. The three types include:

- Threatening.
- Confusing.
- Enhancing.

Threatening

Culture clash is perceived as threatening when a challenge by **others** requires major changes in the fundamental values, attitudes, and behavioral expectations of the organization. Such changes may be as straightforward as offering a new employee benefit or as complex as altering the way employee performance is valued and measured. In each case, the change poses a threat to the traditional "right way" and implies that it is no longer appropriate.

Confusing

Culture clash is perceived as confusing when a challenge to the organization by **others** is not clearly articulated or is difficult to understand. For example, high turnover and resistance to organizational rules by **others** occur in many organizations. Yet, the reasons behind these actions are often unclear or misunderstood by the dominant group. In many cases, those who leave or refuse to comply are blamed for "causing" the problem.

Sometimes, as diversity increases, changes in the physical environment are required; for example, removing pinup calendars from workplace walls in quarters shared by men and women. When this occurs, the rationale is frequently not seen as valid by those asked to make the change. As a result, they often assume that there is something wrong with those who are demanding that the offensive material be removed.

Enhancing

Culture clash can be perceived as enhancing when a challenge to the organization is seen as having the potential to improve effectiveness or positively impact the bottom line. This can occur when **others,** by virtue of their differences, are perceived as better able to communicate with specific constituencies, identify new markets, or provide fresh insights. In such cases, the culture clash is perceived more positively. While the term *clash* implies conflict, the conflict proves to be productive because it helps identify opportunities that had not been considered before.

REACTIONS TO CULTURE CLASH

It is important to recognize that a challenge to the organization culture can often elicit all three types of reactions simultaneously. Furthermore, as the intensity of the conflict ebbs and flows over time, initial reactions change. In cases where challenges are perceived as **threatening,** common reactions among members of the dominant group often include **avoidance, denial,** and **defensiveness.** Occasionally, group members may also exhibit **hostility.** As such, they may attempt to ignore the problem and hope that it goes away. They may also deny that the problem truly exists or become defensive about their own positions and openly hostile towards **others.**

When a challenge is seen as **confusing,** those in the dominant group often **seek or provide more information** or attempt to **redefine the problem.** If members suspect that **others** do not understand them, rather than vice versa, they may attempt to provide additional information to help "clarify" issues. Conversely, they may subconsciously redefine the problem so that it becomes less serious or more consistent with their own values. For example, instead of seeing alleged homophobia as a legitimate workplace issue, members of the mainstream may regard it as oversensitivity on the part of gay men and lesbians.

When culture clash is viewed as **enhancing,** reactions to it often include **heightened anticipation, increased awareness,** and **proaction.** Conscious effort is made by those being challenged to listen to questions posed about the organization culture. Dominant group members recognize that change may increase the organization's effectiveness. As a result of this insight, the conflict becomes energizing and stimulating.

CULTURE CLASH: A CASE HISTORY

While culture clash can be categorized and discussed in the abstract, its dynamic qualities can best be understood in an organizational context. To illustrate the dynamics of culture clash, the authors have chosen to examine the local professional fire service, an institution that has experienced considerable conflict during the past two decades as a result of increased employee diversity.

Historically throughout America, local professional fire departments have been very homogeneous—with white, young, and middle-aged males predominating, no women, few men of color, and no known gay men. Because fire fighting requires round-the-clock coverage, fire fighters tend to work three 24-hour shifts and share common living quarters at most urban fire stations. In addition to fighting fires, they also repair equipment, undergo periodic training, respond to emergency medical calls, and engage in physical fitness activities. While on duty, they eat meals together, sleep in the same quarters, and spend their waking hours together. Off duty, they also tend to socialize together with their families.

Given the hours and the nature of the work performed, fire fighters from the same local station become an extended family. They depend on each other in life threatening situations and, like people in the military who live and work together, then tend to grow very close. Generally, local fire stations also have their own rituals, traditions, and rules for conduct and safety. In this sense, each station is like a small society with a rich history and a highly developed set of expectations and norms. Because the homogeneous ideal has also permeated the culture of the local professional fire station throughout America, it is not surprising that, historically, men of color who became fire fighters were routinely assigned to segregated stations.

Since the passage of the Civil Rights Act of 1964 and the advent of affirmative action, firehouses throughout the United States have been challenged by women and people of color wishing to join these organizations. As more men of color and women have entered the fire service in recent years, their entry has often been viewed by those in the dominant group as threatening and confusing. Rarely has this change been seen as enhancing.

RESPONSES TO THREATENING CULTURE CLASH

One fire service that has experienced considerable culture clash is the Los Angeles City Fire Department—a local department that serves one of the most diverse communities in the United States. Today, within the County of Los Angeles, over 80 languages are spoken by local residents. Virtually every racial and ethnic group in the world is represented within this community.

Prior to the Civil Rights Act of 1964, racial segregation in the Los Angeles Fire Department had become a major issue. Beginning as far back as 1953, when the city's mayor attempted to institute a policy of desegregation, strong opposition to this change was evident—beginning with the Fire Chief himself.[3] As the white male culture of the American firehouse became threatened by the entrance of men of color, reactions from the mainstream invariably included *avoidance, denial, defensiveness,* and *hostility.*

While there were more than 1,700 firefighters in the Los Angeles department in 1953, only 55 were African-Americans. These black fire fighters were all assigned to two stations in the central part of the city—in predominantly black neighborhoods. Although 80 percent of the men assigned to these stations requested transfers, their requests were routinely turned down by the department. This reluctance to desegregate the stations was the Chief's way of avoiding potential culture clash between black and white employees. The department also defended its position by stating that the vast majority of white fire fighters were opposed to desegregation. To support this defense, the department cited the fact that 1,700 of the 1,727 white fire fighters in the department had written letters to the Chief threatening to resign if black employees were assigned to their stations. These letters are evidence of the defensive reaction of the majority of white fire fighters, who saw desegregation as a threat to the sanctity of their "homes away from home."

Although racial attitudes have improved in the Los Angeles Fire Department since 1953, a threatening reaction to increased diversity also occurred in 1988 in a tension-charged San Francisco fire station. This incident centered around the discovery of a swastika in a local station that was experiencing racial tension. It is illustrative of hostile reactions that have occurred in stations throughout the United States, where fire fighters of diverse racial identities are expected to live and work together.

At a packed court hearing on the swastika incident, a federal judge put the San Francisco Chief and 60 officers on notice stating that they would face stiff penalities if they violated a far-reaching court order aimed at unifying the strife-torn department.[4] While an attorney representing women and black fire fighters states that the judge's order "couldn't have come too soon," the president of the local fire fighters union defended the Chief and the department—denying charges that the force was out of control.[5]

The denial of this racially motivated incident in 1988 is not very different from the 1954 denial by the Los Angeles Chief who claimed that desegregation was not needed in the local stations because "integration had not worked satisfactorily in any department," and "since the local station is the fire fighter's home, it is not a place to carry out social experiments."[6] At the time, the Chief went on to defend his position by adding that the stations to which African-American fire fighters were assigned had better than average facilities, thus negating the claim of racial discrimination.

Harassment of Others

Those threatened by a challenge to the dominant culture will sometimes react by harassing **others** in an effort to impede change and preserve the status quo. Within local firehouses, this harassment has taken many distinct forms. Sometimes, the initiation rituals routinely used to induct new recruits are used as a way of embarrassing **others.** For example, in one local firehouse, a woman recruit was asked to perform a demeaning act (which was sexual in nature) as part of the local initiation ritual. When the woman refused, she was informed that she would be treated as an outcast if she did not comply.

Not wishing to be ostracized by her co-workers, she finally relented and performed the ritual. Although she did not lodge a complaint about the incident, someone else in the department chose to tell the Chief. After a full investigation, the male fire fighters involved in the incident were reprimanded and suspended without pay for two days. Shortly thereafter, the woman was transferred to another station.

Arriving at her new "home," she was greeted by a sign soliciting donations from the fire fighters to pay the lost wages of those who had been reprimanded because of the earlier hazing incident. Needless to say, the sign made it clear to the woman that she could expect little support from her colleagues and would remain an outcast in her new surroundings.

Reverse Discrimination

Among the many responses to threatening culture clash, none has gotten more attention in recent years than the claim of "reverse discrimination." Typically, this claim is used to characterize any preference for **others** over those in the dominant group. In applying the concept of reverse discrimination within the local fire station, one cannot help but notice that while historical preferences for white over black fire fighters were widely accepted, the preference for qualified people of color and white women as part of current affirmative action efforts is often deemed "reverse discrimination" by members of the mainstream.

While the term *reverse discrimination* is relatively new, the claim has been used frequently to oppose affirmative action and support dissent and resistance to change within many mainstream organization cultures. First coined by the conservative columnist James Kilpatrick in 1974, the term was later popularized by presidential candidate Ronald Reagan, who stated, "If you belong to an ethnic group not recognized by the federal government as entitled to special treatment, you are a victim of reverse discrimination."[7] Since that time, the term has become a part of the American lexicon.

RESPONSES TO CONFUSING CULTURE CLASH

Some individuals who complain of reverse discrimination use this argument to redefine a problem and make it more acceptable. As such, "reverse discrimination" is a frequent mainstream response to confusing culture clash. Instead of focusing on the historical context of overt discrimination that explains the need for affirmative action today, individuals confused by culture clash often choose to focus only on the "here and now" facts. Thus, taken out of its historical context, affirmative action becomes reverse discrimination.

Another variation on the redefinition theme is the tendency by those attempting to "manage" culture clash to restate a serious problem or incident in less serious terms. Often, this occurs at an unconscious level. A recent occurrence at the U.S. Naval Academy at Annapolis illustrates this point.

In May 1990, a female midshipman resigned from the Academy after two male classmates dragged her from her room, handcuffed her to a urinal, and taunted her as others snapped pictures. On the basis of the publicized facts, the incident appeared to be a clear-cut case of hazing—an offense punishable by dismissal. However, Academy officials ruled that the assault wasn't premeditated and therefore wasn't technically hazing. As a result of this ruling, the eight men involved in the incident got off with written reprimands, demerits, and loss of leave time.

In explaining his decision, the academy superintendent stated, "This escalated from a snowball-throwing incident minutes earlier. So what started out as a good-natured exchange got out of hand. They overstepped a boundary."

In her letter of resignation, the woman cited "very serious human relations problems" within the institution stating that resentment towards the presence of women crushes their spirit. In her case, this male resistance together with the institution's redefinition of the problem caused her to leave.[8]

Another predictable response to confusing culture clash is seeking additional information. A recent incident in another local fire station illustrates this reaction. This incident occurred in a Los Angeles station after a woman paramedic had returned from a rescue call. During the call, she had discovered the mutilated body of a woman who had been raped and murdered. Returning to the fire station, she entered the TV room to find her male colleagues watching a simulated rape in a pornographic film. Distressed by the tragedy that she had just witnessed, the woman walked out—noting that she could not recall a single station she had ever visited where there were no pornographic entertainment materials.[9]

As a result of this incident and complaints from other women in the fire service, the Chief decided to seek additional information about the nature of the problem and ordered a survey to identify all print and video entertainment materials that were available in the station houses. This survey did not attempt to identify the viewing habits of the fire fighters. It simply attempted to inventory available materials. As a result of the survey, the Chief learned that most sexually explicit materials were kept in personal lockers and cabinets. He then asked the city attorney to advise the department on its legal right to restrict the use of sexually explicit entertainment materials. While waiting for the attorney's opinion, the Chief was asked what he thought he might do in response to the problem. He is reported to have said, "If someone wants to read *Playboy* on duty, he can—if he sits inside his locker and shuts the door."[10]

RESPONSES TO ENHANCING CULTURE CLASH

Occasionally, a challenge to the mainstream culture may immediately be seen as enhancing—if it is perceived to improve effectiveness, make the work environment more interesting, more reflective of demographic changes, or more consistent with democratic principles. This reaction is most likely to occur when **others** involved in the culture clash are perceived by those in the mainstream to possess skills needed for improved effectiveness. When this occurs, common reactions from those in the mainstream often include anticipation, heightened awareness, and proaction. Once again, the Los Angeles Fire Department serves as an example.

In 1978, before there were women fire fighters in Los Angeles, Ann Reiss Lane was president of the local Fire Commission—the agency that oversees the governance of the department and local fire stations. Although she lacked experience as a fire fighter, the commissioner recognized that fire fighting was a profession women should be encouraged to pursue. She believed that barriers to entering the profession should be work-related, not gender-related. An expression often used in the local firehouses at the time, that "men fight fires and women make babies," did not reflect her personal sentiments.

In 1982, anticipating that women would want to become fire fighters if given any encouragement, the commissioner insisted that the department develop a program to prepare them to enter the fire service. As a result, a dispatch station was converted into an exercise gym and a weight training coach was hired to work with the women recruits. An outreach program to interest women in the profession was also put in place and orientations were held on a quarterly basis to explain the job and interest women in applying for the position. As a result of this aggressive effort to attract women, there are now 77 women fire fighters and paramedics in the Los Angeles department. By becoming more aware of what supplemental training was needed to help women qualify and proactively recruiting and developing women to meet the department's work standards, the Los Angeles Fire Department enlarged its own candidate pool without sacrificing professionalism or downgrading standards. Its success in this area has made the local department a model for others across the United States.

The story of the Los Angeles Fire Department's various reactions to culture clash—from threatening to confusing to enhancing—is far from unique. In fact, similar culture clashes have occurred and continue to occur in every sector of the American workplace. As more organizations begin to recognize the added value that **others** can offer in identifying new business opportunities, relating to diverse customers, and solving productivity problems, the more likely it is that future culture clash will be viewed as enhancing. The example of enhancing culture clash within the fire department points out that organizations that historically viewed changes in their workforce as threatening can learn to react more productively—with the help of enlightened leadership.

When asked how he viewed the changes generated by the influx of **others** into the Los Angeles Fire Department, its current Chief, Donald Manning, recently said: "There is strength in heterogeneity. When there is inbreeding or homogeneity in an organization, it loses its ability to be objective—to meet the needs of a diverse community." Given the enormous diversity that exists within Los Angeles, the local fire department simply had to change to serve the community—and change it has.

Japanese Automaking in America

One of the best examples of enhancing culture clash to take place during the past decade occurred when several Japanese automobile manufacturers decided to establish production facilities within the United States. By the early 80s, the American auto industry was in serious decline. Domestic market share was plunging. The Japanese were universally recognized to be manufacturing the world's highest quality products on the most advanced assembly lines.

In an effort to infuse new skills into a stagnant industry and new jobs into a recession economy, state and local government groups negotiated with Nissan, Mazda, and Toyota to build plants in this country. Invariably, the small cities slated as sites for these new operations awaited their arrival with a mixture of excitement and apprehension. American workers needed the jobs and training, but they were unsure of what to expect from organizations out of a culture so different from their own. For their part, the Japanese weren't certain that their proven management techniques could be successfully transported across the Pacific.

Predictably, there was a learning phase in which the two cultures came together, heightened awareness, and made mutual adjustments. In this proactive process of "give and take," concessions were usually made by both employees and management. For example, American workers declined union affiliation in return for more competitive wages and the promise of lifetime employment. The Japanese abandoned such practices as morning exercise programs that seemed inconsistent with American routines.[11] More importantly, when subjected to early criticism about discriminatory hiring policies, the organizations stepped up efforts to hire more diverse employees.

Today, 10 years later, evidence suggests that the experiment has been successful. The culture clash has been enhancing for both the automakers and plant employees. As one recent article in *Fortune* stated:

> The Japanese plants are an overwhelming plus when it comes to advancing the manufacturing art. And along with installing some of the latest machinery, Japan's automakers are inculcating American workers with radically different attitudes. . . .
>
> Even the newest hires are made to feel important. They participate in decisions that American plants usually leave to management, such as scheduling overtime or rotating jobs. Many seem almost like converts to a new religion. As one American associate in Honda's body-stamping shop

puts it, "For once in my life, I've got something to believe in."[12]

THE EVOLUTION OF CULTURE CLASH

As we've seen in many of the examples discussed in this chapter, culture clash is not static—it tends to evolve over time. For this reason, any single strategy for managing culture clash is not likely to succeed over a prolonged period. Instead, as the response to culture clash evolves, the strategies used to manage culture clash must also evolve.

Public accounting is an example of an industry that has been forced to consider many strategies to manage culture clash over time. Historically, like fire departments, accounting firms have relied on a largely white male professional group to meet their staffing needs. And like most professions, accounting has long had a homogeneous ideal that accountants are expected to emulate.

Among the qualities associated with this ideal type is the ability to generate new business through social contacts. To accomplish this, many CPAs routinely meet with their clients, peers, and associates for lunch, drinks, dinner, a round of golf, and so on. They understand that promotions to partner and managing partner are often based on the strength of one's social relationships both within and outside the firm. However, for many women CPAs, breaking into these social circles has been an exceedingly difficult task since many claim "they are hardly ever invited to golf outings where partners prove their mettle in bringing in business."[13]

In the early 1980s, as more women joined accounting firms, this exclusion from the male social network was the first sign of gender-related culture clash. The second sign came when women began organizing their own professional groups in order to network and discuss issues of common concern. While some firms responded by denying the need for these organizations, a few recognized the exclusionary nature of their organizational cultures. They believed that women CPAs could enhance their firms' ability to compete for new business and took steps to include them in social outings with potential clients.

One firm even acknowledged that golf wasn't the only activity that could be used to build social contacts. Because this tended to be the preferred sport of men but not of most women CPAs, client outings were arranged to appeal to a range of diverse interests such as tennis, theater, and good conversation. Not surprisingly, this firm discovered that the change was welcomed by many clients—as well as by women employees.

As many women CPAs began rejecting navy skirt suits and bow ties in favor of more feminine attire, some of their male colleagues reacted with confusion—unable to recognize the significance of the traditional, male-oriented "uniform." Eventually, some organizations responded by relaxing the informal dress code to accommodate this difference.

Today, based on a growing bottom-line need to recruit and retain women accountants, many accounting firms have begun to alter traditional work schedules, leave policies, and so on in order to support the needs of a more diverse workforce. While the mass entrance of women is widely acknowledged to be the impetus behind such changes, the result will be an enhanced work environment that acknowledges a wider range of interests and needs that exists among *all* employees.

Moving from Threat and Confusion to Enhancement

Of the many variables that help to characterize a culture clash as threatening, confusing, or enhancing, none is more predictive of the dominant group's reactions than the value attributed to **others.** In cases where the dominant group perceives that the inclusion of **others** has little value to them or the organization, the likelihood of threatening culture clash is extremely high. In cases where the value of diversity is unknown, confusion and data gathering are often the result. However, in those instances where the dominant group recognizes the added value that **others** bring to complex tasks like problem analysis and service to diverse customers, culture clash is most likely to be viewed as enhancing and to be managed in a productive, win-win manner.

In enhancing situations, the ability to develop creative solutions to culture clash is *greater* among members of the dominant group than is true in threatening or confusing situations. This ability to find new solutions has little to do with the complexity of the perceived problem. Instead, it is directly related to the value ascribed to **others**. In enhancing situations, dominant group members associate some personal or organizational benefit with accepting and supporting increased diversity. As a result, they are more motivated to find new methods, make needed changes, and less inclined to defend against change or blame **others**.

This pattern, which exists throughout organizations in the American workplace, suggests that threatening and confusing culture clash can be minimized when diversity is understood and valued. Therefore, institutions that position diversity as a positive change, rather than a regrettable yet unavoidable one, will be the ultimate beneficiaries. They will not only succeed in attracting the best and brightest from the increasingly diverse U.S. labor pool, they will also experience less difficulty managing the organizational transition from assimilation to valuing diversity. While there will be inevitable culture clash, it is more likely to lead to enhancements and less likely to generate threat and confusion.

NOTES

1. Elizabeth Kristol, "False Tolerance, False Unity," *New York Times*, September 25, 1989, p. 19.
2. Marilyn Loden, *Feminine Leadership or How to Succeed in Business without Being One of the Boys* (New York: Times Books, 1985), p. 26.
3. Frank Sherwood and Beatrice Markey, *The Mayor and the Fire Chief: The Fight over Integrating the Los Angeles Fire Department* #43 (University, Alabama: University of Alabama Press, January, 1958), p. 1.
4. Leslie Guevarra and Dawn Garcia, "Judge Says Fire Department Is 'Out of Control' in San Francisco," *San Francisco Chronicle*, January 15, 1988, pp. A1–2.
5. Ibid.
6. Hartsfield-Mills, A. B., *The Old Stentorians* (Santa Fe Springs, Calif.: Stockton Trade Press, 1973), p. 56.
7. Jon Nordheimer, "Reagan Attacks Carter as Vague," *New York Times*, July 7, 1978, p. 14.
8. "Woman Harassed at Naval Academy," *San Francisco Chronicle*, May 14, 1990, p. A3.

9. John Kendall, "Sexually Explicit Material in Firehouses: Trying to Douse a Blazing Issue," *Los Angeles Times*, February 14, 1988, pp. 1–2.

10. Ibid., pp. 1–2.

11. Louis Kraar, "Japan's Gung-Ho U.S. Car Plants," *Fortune*, January 30, 1989, p. 106.

12. Ibid., p. 100.

13. Eric C. Berg, "The Big Eight: Still a Male Bastion," *New York Times*, July 12, 1988, p. D1, D7.

Chapter Eight

Establishing Common Ground

"America is not a blanket, woven from one thread, one color, one cloth. When I was a child in South Carolina and momma couldn't afford a blanket . . . she took pieces of old cloth—wool, silk, gabardine, croker sack—only patches, barely good enough to shine your shoes with. But they didn't stay that way long. With sturdy hands and strong cord, she sewed them together into a quilt, a thing of power, beauty and culture. Now we must build a quilt together."[1]

The Reverend Jesse Jackson, Social Activist and U.S. Presidential Candidate

A mong the rationales used to support the value of assimilation, none is more popular than the "Tower of Babel" argument. Like the biblical story in which people speaking different languages are unable to communicate or coordinate their efforts, this argument presumes that the philosophy of valuing diversity will inevitably lead to a breakdown in standards and quality control. According to the proponents of this view, as institutions acknowledge more stylistic differences and work to accommodate the values and perspectives of **others,** they will no longer be able to distinguish "good performance" from "bad" or "acceptable behavior" from "unacceptable." Ultimately, this breakdown in standards will lead to anarchy and total subjectivity—making it impossible for organizations to "objectively" reward or discipline employees.

Anyone who has ever attempted to introduce institutional reform of any kind will not be surprised by this argument. It is a predictable response that routinely occurs when organizations are confronted with the need to change. Although one cannot prevent the reaction from occurring, it is still useful to anticipate its coming—in order to diminish any potential negative impact on efforts aimed at valuing diversity.

While today's managers must focus on the importance of valuing human differences in order to succeed, it is *also* true that they require a set of universal principles to help coalesce, coordinate, and direct the actions of *all* employees. In other words, there is the simultaneous need for greater differentiation *and* greater common ground. Acknowledging this seeming paradox in the philosophy of valuing diversity is a simple but important first step that can often help allay fears of change.

DEFINING COMMON GROUND

Whether one's goal is enhanced productivity, bottom-line profit, or effective human resources management, establishing common ground is critical in organizations that value diversity. By **common ground** we mean **a shared set of assumptions that provide the basis for all cooperative action.** More precisely, common ground must include: shared goals, shared rewards, mutual respect and understanding, mutual commitment to fairness, and a shared vision of the future. Like the U.S. constitution that provides the framework for democratic action, common ground is the social contract endorsed by every employee within the organization.

In the future, as organizations continue to become more diverse, common ground will become more necessary for effective functioning. For without commonly accepted principles to guide employee action, diversity has the potential to become an unruly and divisive force. Without common ground, many **others** are likely to become "majority minorities" in U.S. institutions—with little influence and little stake in the future of the organization. As such, it will be unrealistic for managers to expect more than a minimum effort from **others** in organizations that do not recognize or support their talents, aspirations, and needs.

Once basic operating principles that respect diversity are articulated, the standards used to evaluate and measure employee performance must then evolve out of these common principles. In many organizations, new standards encouraging a broad range of stylistic differences will be required—for organizations cannot say "we value diversity" and still measure people by the traditional white male yardstick. While valuing diversity will require enlarging the range of acceptable behavior, it will *not* require that institutions abandon standards needed to evaluate and reward employees performance. Instead, some standards will change—to reflect the wider range of talents and styles that exist within the organization.

As the workforce grows increasingly diverse, the need to articulate core organizational values, operating principles, and performance standards that allow for stylistic differences *also* increases. However, unilateral actions aimed at establishing these core values and operating principles will not be successful. To be effective, the development of common values and standards requires input from diverse sources. To become common ground, these principles ultimately need the endorsement and ongoing support of diverse employees at all levels of the organization.

COMMON GROUND: MYTH VERSUS REALITY

To work effectively together, all individuals need a common sense of purpose and a shared commitment to organizational goals. This shared sense of purpose is a critical requirement in every group—regardless of how diverse it may be. In the past, creating a shared sense of purpose appeared to be a less complicated task. In most organizations, it simply required getting **others** to accept the values and perspectives of the dominant group.

Today, institutions are beginning to realize that the myth of assimilation and the imposition of the dominant group's values on **others** does not create the reality of a common sense of purpose. While most could live with the consequences of this imposed action in the past, no organization in America can afford to continue this practice in the future. Improved productivity, quality, and market sensitivity will not allow for it. Instead of imposing mainstream values on **others,** organizations are beginning to recognize the importance of building commitment among all employees based on a solid foundation of true common ground.

Developing a common sense of purpose is a complex process in organizations that value diversity. It is also more *possible* than it has ever been—because, for the first time, organizations recognize that it requires "buy-in" from many diverse groups. Today, in institutions throughout America, one can see a philosophical progression taking place away from **assimilation** as a strategy for managing diversity towards greater **differentiation** and, finally, to true **integration.** This philosophical progression is essential in organizations intent on establishing common ground.

THE PATH TO COMMON GROUND

Although some institutions still do not acknowledge the failure of assimilation to productively manage diversity, more are beginning to recognize the inherent limitations of this strategy. In corporations, government offices, and universities, evidence of the shortcomings of assimilation has been mounting in recent years. During the last two decades, as women, people of color, older employees, lesbians, gay men, and **others** became disenchanted with the inhospitable culture of their organizations, many chose to drop out. Those who remained often wound up giving less than 100 percent of their energy to their work because of resentment and cynicism. As a consequence, many organizations experienced a noticeable "brain drain" during the late 70s and throughout the 80s, as **others** with talent and potential moved out or shut down.[2]

Today, we see more institutions embracing the philosophy of valuing diversity to stop this brain drain and create a more supportive, flexible work environment. As they abandon the strategy of assimilation, these organizations are encouraging greater differentiation among employees of diverse core identities. Unlike the past, efforts to define and differentiate **otherness** are now being encouraged, not discouraged. Employee education to raise awareness of diversity issues and increase mutual respect is also being provided as a matter of course.

While this emphasis on increased diversity is a positive step in the change process, it is not the final step. For greater differentiation does not equate with true integration. For integration to occur, employees of diverse core identities must also recognize the need for and establish common ground. They must become "a part of" rather than remain "apart from" the mainstream culture. To become part of the mainstream, **others** must have an increasingly active role in shaping the culture. As such, the mainstream culture must become the **culture of diversity** and operate off a set of guiding principles that every individual—regardless of core identity—can support.

To date, most institutional change efforts to value diversity have focused primarily on employee education *without* examining the ways in which organizational values and practices may need to change. While education can do much to enhance interpersonal relations, it cannot change systems that delimit **others**. Education can help individuals move from assimilation to differentiation as a strategy for managing diversity. However, it cannot create integrated organizations that reflect the values and experiences of all diverse members. To create the culture of diversity, a sustained, systematic approach is required.

A Journey in Progress

Virtually no organization in America is a truly integrated organization today. To be integrated, institutions must evolve beyond differentiation, establishing common ground, and transforming their cultures to accommodate key dimensions of diversity. They must be managed and staffed by diverse people who understand and respect core differences. They must have systems in place that reward excellent performance—regardless of the size, shape, age, affectional orientation, or color of the performer. When the value of diversity is no longer discussed in the abstract, is no longer challenged, misinterpreted, or viewed as a threat, but, instead, is expressed in tangible benefits for employees and their employers, then common ground and true integration will become realities.

As Larry Waller, diversity consultant and retired director of pluralism at U S West stated in a recent interview for this book:

> Fifteen years ago, a few U.S. companies embarked on a mission to raise corporate consciousness about race and gender issues. Today, the companies that stuck with this educational effort, have moved beyond assimilation. Some have reached the stage where employees no longer have to fit the old mold. But even in these organizations, integration is still a future goal. While things are starting to change, the character and climate in these companies still disproportionately favors the attitudes, experiences and behaviors of white men.

Based on initial efforts to establish common ground occurring within some organizations, it is evident that this transformation process is complex and time-consuming. While some may argue that the potential return is not worth the considerable effort required, common ground is essential for organization survival. For without it, no U.S. institution will be positioned to attract, retain, and maximize the talents and creative potential of diverse employees, relate to diverse customers, or compete in the global marketplace.

KEY STEPS ALONG THE WAY

In organizations already working to establish common ground, the defined scope of this change effort is an early predictor of failure and success. Where the scope is limited to education, benefit enhancements, or revised work rules, minimal culture change is occurring. Where efforts are more comprehensive and simultaneously address the needs for education, procedural changes, sustained senior management support, and so on, greater progress is being made. Although no organization has completed the task of establishing common ground, some are continuing to move towards a culture of diversity in which employees respect differences, pursue common goals, and operate under mutually agreed to principles. In these organizations, several important initiatives are now occurring. These include:

(1) Acknowledging the limitations of assimilation as a strategy for managing employee diversity.

(2) Adopting the philosophy of valuing diversity and encouraging greater employee differentiation.

(3) Increasing employee awareness of cultural differences and similarities.

(4) Leveraging differences for improved productivity, enhanced customer relations, and increased profit.

(5) Redefining relationships between **others** and members of the dominant group.

(6) Developing collaborative alliances based on cultural similarities and differences, common needs, and interests.

(7) Reducing cultural bias in performance standards.

(8) Aligning organizational objectives with the emerging culture of diversity.

Acknowledging the Limitations of Assimilation

No institution can establish common ground by simultaneously paying lip service to the value of diversity while imposing the values of the dominant group on **others.** When this occurs, regardless of the tone of the rhetoric, assimilation continues to be reinforced as a core organizational value. In organizations committed to culture change, managers and employees are learning to "walk the talk" of diversity by demonstrating support through actions. Within these institutions, employees at every level recognize that assimilation is an out-of-date strategy for managing human resources. They understand that assimilation was an important part of the organization's history but also realize it must now be replaced with a new strategy that will utilize the skills of all employees.

To create the impetus for change, employees must first recognize why the strategy of assimilation is breaking down. They must become aware of the ways in which assimilation stifles energy, creativity, and commitment among **others** and recognize the importance of the paradigm shift away from assimilation towards greater differentiation. As such, acknowledgment of the limitations of assimilation is a key insight that must be shared by managers and employees in organizations intent on establishing common ground.

Adopting the Philosophy of Valuing Diversity

When the limitations of assimilation are acknowledged throughout the organization, an appropriate context for introducing the philosophy of valuing diversity is created. Without this formal acknowledgement, the need for a change in strategy is less clear and the organization's commitment to this new philosophy is less apparent.

Some organizations choose not to acknowledge the inherent limitations of assimilation and, instead, point to changing workforce demographics as the impetus behind the move to valuing diversity. However, to diverse employees who recognize that core differences have always existed, this explanation can create resentment and cynicism. "When it was a moral issue, they didn't care. Now that it's an economic one, they're worried about the bottom line but not the employees," is a sentiment expressed by many **others** in organizations that ignore or sidestep the issue of assimilation.

To be accepted and endorsed by **others,** the value of diversity must be placed in a realistic context. It must be treated as a positive step in a long-term change process away from assimilation towards integration. Where the impact of assimilation is used to frame the adoption of this new strategy, an appropriate context is created within the organization. Where valuing diversity is not linked to assimilation, it is often perceived as a less powerful change strategy and loses credibility with **others.** It becomes the right solution being implemented for insufficient reason, causing many employees to ask, "What's really in it for us?"

Increasing Awareness of Cultural Similarities and Differences

As with any significant organizational change, the philosophical shift from assimilation to valuing diversity inevitably requires changes in behavior among most managers and employees. Yet, unlike technological changes that are routinely supported by education and retraining, this change is often introduced without addressing the serious skill deficiencies that exist at every level of the organization. While the concept of valuing diversity is simple to understand, appropriate actions required to support this philosophy are often subtle and difficult to develop without coaching and personal feedback. In many cases, these skills are missing from employees' behavioral repertoires.

In organizations committed to establishing common ground, manager and employee retraining to support the value of diversity is viewed as an essential part of the change process. Just as these organizations would not expect an untrained employee to operate a sophisticated piece of equipment without training, they do not assume that managers and employees have the personal awareness and the skills necessary to manage and deal with employee diversity as a vital resource.

Establishing common ground requires that employees of all core identities become more familiar and more comfortable with **others.** As such, the diversity paradox or the idea that people are different *and* the same is an important part of educational efforts to support diversity. Without a deeper appreciation of human similarities and core differences, cultural myopia will usually prevail in the workplace—even among those who accept the philosophy of valuing diversity. This all too human tendency to judge **others** by one's own cultural standards is an issue that can best be addressed in group training.

By learning about cultural and stylistic differences in a group setting, employees can better understand the behavior of **others** without judging or stereotyping it. They can develop a new perspective that acknowledges core differences and human similarities. As King-Ming Young, manager of diversity at Hewlett-Packard Company stated in a recent interview: "The way to color blindess is through color-consciousness."[3] As such, employees must recognize and respect core differences before they can deal with **others** in a nonjudgmental manner. Appreciating that people of diverse cultural backgrounds also *share* the same fundamental needs for acceptance, recognition, and support can help build more trusting, human connections among diverse employees. As these connections develop, the value of differences and the need for common ground become more evident.

Leveraging Differences

Some individuals argue that valuing diversity is a moral imperative; others assert that it is an economic one. In essence, both arguments create a false dichotomy and miss the main point. The point is that the philosophy of valuing diversity is both morally and economically essential for the American workplace of the future. One of the most empowering aspects of this essential change is the obvious opportunity for growth and development that it offers to everyone. In this case, literally everybody wins.

In institutions intent on establishing common ground, the dichotomy of morality versus economics is recognized as false. Instead of debating the point, managers and employees recognize the tremendous leverage that valuing diversity offers to everyone. As such, managers work to increase diversity within their organizations—recognizing that while it offers **others** increased opportunity, it also offers the institution more creative potential. **Otherness** is viewed as a unique asset that can add rich new perspectives to the resources of the work group and help organizations understand the needs of diverse customers. As James E. Preston, president and chief operating officer of Avon Products, Inc., stated: "We are consumer marketers and the marketplace is very diverse in this country. Who best understands the needs of Hispanics, Asians, and women than Hispanics, Asians, and women?"[4]

In addition to addressing diverse market needs, increased diversity can also make the workplace more spirited, stimulating, and productive. As employees interact with **others** on a regular basis, their own experiences provide living testimony about the value of diversity. Comments such as, "She got that job to fill a quota" are seldom heard. Instead, one is more likely to hear observations like, "She's really brought something new to the party!"

Redefining Relationships among Others

Until managers and employees acknowledge interpersonal and intergroup conflicts, develop a multicultural perspective, and experience increased comfort working with **others,** most can be expected to resist organizational efforts aimed at establishing common ground. Given our collective history dealing with **otherness,** this should not be surprising. Because of the failure of our society to value diversity and the failure of most institutions to manage diversity as an asset, many employees now view common ground as an unrealistic goal. Too much effort has been spent reinforcing assimilation and the values of the dominant group for **others** to be easily convinced that much is going to change now.

Yet, many forces at work in America are making this change a real possibility—perhaps for the first time. Unlike the past, when social change was created through legislative initiative, today it is the American workplace that recognizes the need for change and has the human and economic resources required to bring this change about. It is in the American workplace that historical relationships between those in the mainstream and those outside can and *must* finally change.

In organizations committed to establishing common ground, employees of diverse core identities are beginning to recognize the necessity of redefining their relationships with **others.** For members of dominant groups, such as white people, men, heterosexual people, physically able-bodied people, and so on, this redefinition of relationships requires recognition of the inherent equality of **others.** It means abandoning dominance in favor of pluralism—the belief that all primary and secondary human differences can coexist, complement each other, and contribute to the greater good.

Given our societal history, the major responsibility for changing relationships and establishing common ground now rests with those who are dominant in organizations—not only because they have the power required to create change but because they alone can overcome the suspicion and mistrust of **others** through sincere, sustained commitment to productive action. Once again, it is pointless to argue whether the motivation of the dominant group should be moral or economic. If U.S. institutions are to survive and prosper in the future, if quality in products and services is to remain a principle objective, if increasing global market share is to be a goal in consumer-oriented businesses, then these relationships must change.

As commitment grows and becomes more evident among those who have been dominant historically, **others** will also need to redefine their roles in light of this change. In particular, victim-oppressor metaphors that once accurately described relationships between **others** and the dominant group will need to be abandoned in favor of new definitions characterized by greater trust, interdependence, and cooperation. For some **others** who have lived their lives defining themselves as victims and relating to those in the dominant group as oppressors, this change will be extremely difficult. For regardless of how limiting they may have been, it is never easy to abandon old roles.

In addition, individuals serious about finding common ground will have to give up all claims to moral superiority—claims sometimes made by oppressed **others** in the past. The roles of victim and oppressor will both be outmoded ways of seeing the world and relating to **others** in organizations that succeed in establishing common ground. There will be no need to compete for the title of most oppressed or morally superior. Instead, the culture of the organization and the ongoing actions of managers and employees will finally dispel the need for this.

Obviously, as a society, we have yet to reach this point. Nonetheless, the need for establishing common ground is evident in organizations throughout America, and signs of positive change are becoming more visible. For this change to finally occur, every employee in the American workplace will ultimately have to step towards **others**—letting go of the suspicion and mistrust of the past as a prerequisite for building a better future together.

Developing Collaborative Alliances

In the future, as more employees redefine and strengthen their relationships with **others,** many will form collaborative partnerships aimed at increased workplace equity and the elimination of stereotyping and the destructive "isms." These alliances will cross the boundaries of core differences. They will be composed of diverse employees who recognize their own interdependence and who are willing to work together to lobby for continued change.

At this stage, ageism, heterosexism, racism, and so on, will no longer be regarded as the primary concerns of victims or of **others.** Instead, employees of all core identities will be committed to eliminating the vestiges of these destructive "isms" from the workplace and society at large. Because majority groups will continue to change as diversity increases in the American workplace, pluralism—the coexistence of many cultures within a society—will be an increasingly appropriate model for understanding the makeup, distribution of influence, and governance of diverse organizations. Majority versus minority paradigms will become increasingly inappropriate— as employees cross ethnic, affectional orientation, age, racial, and gender lines to form new majorities and common interest alliances.

Reducing Cultural Bias in Performance Standards

Once the voices of diverse **others** are heard throughout the organization, their increasing influence is likely to lead to an in-depth reexamination of traditional performance standards. Where there is evidence of strong cultural bias, these standards are likely to require redefinition. In order to set more inclusive, unbiased standards, considerable debate and discussion will be required. Ultimately, substantive performance issues will need to be separated from stylistic perferences.

While the sorting process may be uncomfortable at times and conflict over what standards to apply will be inevitable, this debate will be a key step in the transformation of the culture into one that values diversity *as well as* quality performance. As awareness of **otherness** increases within the mainstream culture, the culture itself will be transformed, adapting more readily and naturally to greater diversity. Ultimately, the importance of employee diversity will evolve from a peripheral component of the mainstream culture to a central component. At the same time, performance standards will reflect the cultural diversity of the workplace.

Aligning Organizational Objectives with the Culture of Diversity

To create a culture of diversity, managers, employees, and organizations must first establish common ground. This common ground then becomes the foundation for the new culture of diversity—and supports the standards that are then developed to measure employee and organizational performance. Establishing common ground is a dynamic process, not a static one. In the future, as the organization encounters new competitive and environmental forces that challenge its effective functioning, the shared goals and shared vision that make up this common ground must evolve—in response to changing opportunities and emerging issues. If not, they will eventually become as out-of-date as the philosophy of assimilation is today.

However, this evolution cannot occur at the expense of the original, primary purpose behind establishing common ground—to maximize the voice, stake, and productivity of every employee in the organization. To assure that common ground is maintained once it is discovered, organizational goals and objectives will need to be continuously aligned with the emerging culture of diversity. In cases where objectives appear to be in opposition to the values and operating principles of the new culture, managers and employees will have to consider how to modify these objectives to achieve financial and productivity gains without undermining the organization's shared values, goals, and vision.

DETOURS AND WRONG TURNS

Within complex organizations, efforts to establish common ground among diverse employees can be derailed for many reasons. While some derailment issues have already been identified, several warrant further discussion. These issues include:

- Inappropriate sequencing.
- Insufficient resource allocation.
- Lack of executive education.
- Premature resolution of conflicts.
- Peripheral versus mainstream culture change.

Inappropriate Sequencing

As discussed earlier, moving from assimilation to integration in an organization results from an evolutionary, three-phase change process. This process requires the development of increased cultural awareness among managers and employees during the second or differentiation phase. When organizations attempt to move directly from assimilation to integration, skipping this middle step, employees are deprived of opportunities to explore core differences, become more comfortable interacting with **others,** and acquire the knowledge and heightened sensitivity required to value diversity and manage it as an asset.

While they may support integration as a concept, managers and employees are generally not prepared to relate to **others** in ways that make it an institutional reality. In addition, because of this lack of focus on diversity issues, **others** continue to be "unknowns" to members of the mainstream as well as to other diverse employees. Their values, attitudes, and communication styles remain obscured. Hence, while their numbers may increase within the organization, their status and influence will not necessarily increase at the same rate.

In many organizations that practice participative management and value employee involvement and empowerment, cultural differentiation is viewed as an unnecessary step in the move towards greater "jointness." In fact, some argue that emphasizing group differences will only lead to further stereotyping. These institutions believe diverse work teams that emphasize employee empowerment and joint problem-solving automatically learn how to value diversity through their day-to-day interactions.

Because stereotyping is a programmed, semiautomatic response to **otherness,** it cannot be overlooked or regarded as a

problem that will "take care of itself." Without greater awareness of core differences, the probability of collusion and stereotyping within diverse work teams is enormous. Even within
teams that value listening, collaboration, and empowerment,
cultural filters are still operative. As such, the likelihood that
"jointness" will indirectly address the need for greater respect
and understanding among diverse employees is extremely low
and simply not happening in most institutions in America.

Insufficient Resource Allocation

Because the strategy of assimilation and the homogeneous
ideal are deeply embedded in most organization cultures, efforts to change these cultures and institutionalize the philosophy of valuing diversity take considerable problem analysis,
planning, education, and systems change. It is never a fast or a
simple process.

Today, given the short-term focus of most large organizations in America, the philosophy of valuing diversity is often
seen as a change effort that must be shortened and simplified
for ease of implementation. In such cases, activities are
planned and goals are set to measure "culture change" in a
matter of months or, at the outside, in one to two years.

Within organizations looking for a "quick fix," valuing diversity is usually treated as a fad or short-range approach to re-
lieving tensions created by increased employee diversity. Goals
are set to emphasize immediate results and do not allow
for deeper, systemic change. Financial allocations to support
the change process are also based on immediate return on investment. As such, long-term change is neither discussed nor
supported by the organization's efforts. Instead, because of insufficient allocations of time, people, and dollars, failure to establish common ground and create culture change is built in
from the beginning.

In organizations committed to finding common ground and
changing the mainstream culture, meaningful progress is measured over several years rather than several months. A variety
of resources, including internal change agents, sufficient fi-
nancing, and senior executive commitment, are dedicated to
the effort. While these organizations also monitor the short-

term impact of their change efforts, they recognize that fundamental culture change will not be evident for several years. Therefore, they avoid emphasizing achievement of short-term goals as justification for continuing the project and, instead, set realistic short-term expectations that do not undermine the overall effort.

Lack of Executive Education

A common derailment issue in many organizations intent on culture change is a general lack of education and awareness development at the top. Rather than address the need for additional insight and information at all levels of the organization, change agents in some institutions assume those in senior management have no knowledge gap. Thus, by dint of their positions in the hierarchy, they are exempt from organizational efforts to educate managers and employees about diversity issues.

Instead of receiving more education as leaders of the organization, senior executives in many institutions receive little or none. As a result, it becomes increasingly difficult for members of this group to support or stay connected to the organizational change effort as it builds momentum and grass roots interest over time.

Eventually, this knowledge gap between those at the top and other employees in the organization can become a major source of conflict and culture clash as employees attempt to support organizational change and executives unconsciously thwart their efforts. Conversely, in those organizations experiencing greater success changing their cultures, senior management is generally committed and enlightened about core differences and key diversity issues.

Premature Resolution of Conflicts

While increased awareness can lead to greater acceptance and respect over the long term, it will often surface latent organizational issues and create more conflict in the short term. For example, the introduction of sexual harassment prevention seminars aimed at reducing the number of such incidents in an organization, often triggers an increase in the actual number of formal complaints following training. Because these seminars signal employees that sexual harassment will no longer be tolerated, many previously unknown incidents tend to be reported for the first time. While this increase in complaints indicates there is often a bigger problem than previously known, it does not necessarily mean that the problem of sexual harassment will continue to grow over time. Instead, if appropriate follow-up action is taken to reprimand the offenders, the number of incidents and complaints will usually begin to decline.

Similarly, when awareness training aimed at reducing the impact of personal prejudices and the destructive "isms" is offered in an organization, the initial result may be that many employees become more aware of specific behavior problems and their impact on productivity and morale. Because they are now more aware and no longer willing to collude, these employees will often challenge organizational practices and management behavior that was previously tolerated. They may even embarrass senior management as they do this.

For example, at an annual employee meeting in a large automotive manufacturing plant in the Midwest, the vice president of quality was recently challenged by a member of the audience for referring to women employees at the plant as "girls." Catching himself as he spoke, the V.P. noted that the term "girl" was "a basic part of my socialization. I don't think I can purge it from my vocabulary at this late stage in my career."

While it would have been easy for the audience to let the comment slide, one manager chose to publicly challenge the V.P.'s remarks. Stating that "I, too, have had to check myself and my language," the manager, another white man, went on to say, "Changing our behavior is something we all have to be prepared to do—even those of us who sit at the top."

There is little doubt that most managers and institutions must be prepared to weather many internal storms on the journey towards establishing common ground. Unfortunately, some are not prepared to manage the inevitable controversy that results from a culture change that supports diversity over assimilation. Instead of expecting debate and controversy, there is shock and surprise expressed by those shepherding the change effort when conflict emerges. Senior managers may become distressed over strong negative reactions expressed by various employee groups. The entire change process may actually appear to be coming apart.

At such times, the temptation must be resisted to resolve conflicts quickly or to abandon the change effort entirely. It is far more productive to clearly define the issues at stake, giving all stakeholders ample time to discuss and understand these *before* moving towards resolution. While the discomfort created by conflict may be difficult for many to tolerate, premature resolution of disputes over standards, policy changes, and other key issues can lead to derailment of the entire effort.

Peripheral versus Mainstream Culture Change

While many organizations talk about the need for changing the mainstream culture and establishing shared goals and a shared vision, most stop short of actually doing this. Instead, in most institutions, the dominant group will attempt to appease **others** by making minor changes in operating procedures, announcing a few additional promotions, serving "ethnic" foods in the cafeteria on Tuesdays, or appointing a special task force to "study" diversity issues.

Needless to say, the end result of this appeasement is that the mainstream culture does not change substantively. For awhile, people may talk more about the value of diversity. There may be more management training on the subject. There may even be more than the usual number of promotions of **others,** but the homogeneous ideal lives on. Along with assimilation, it remains embedded within the fabric or culture of the organization.

To date, few U.S. institutions have thought seriously about what is required to truly change the mainstream culture and establish common ground. Since the requirements are considerable, this is not surprising. Yet, throughout America, the workplace shows signs of an increasingly desperate need for change and renewal. Given today's need for improved productivity, profitability, and market sensitivity, can we afford to ignore diversity issues and continue to assume that what has worked in the past will meet our needs in the future? Can we ignore the brain drain that continues to plague many organizations unable to manage **others** effectively? Can we ignore the conflicts that occur each day among employees who lack an understanding of cultural differences?

While most institutions have yet to respond to these questions, some are stepping up to the challenges and discovering the opportunities that culture change can offer. These are organizations with a clear focus on the future and the insight required to plan for inevitable change. In the final section of this book, we will look more closely at these pioneering organizations and their efforts to establish common ground and create cultures of diversity.

NOTES

1. "1988 Democratic National Convention; Jackson: Our Challenge . . . Is to Find Common Ground," Part 1, *Los Angeles Times*, July 20, 1988, p. 6.
2. Loden, Marilyn, "A Machismo that Drives Women Out," *New York Times*, February 9, 1986, p. D–1.
3. Jolie Solomon, "Firms Address Workers' Cultural Variety," *The Wall Street Journal*, February 10, 1989, p. B1.
4. Sharon Nelton, "Meet Your New Workforce," *Nation's Business*, July 1988, p. 16.

PART
III

Diversity and Organization Change

Chapter Nine

Valuing Diversity in Leading–Edge Organizations

"In the valuing diversity company, you see employees who are less risk averse, who play to win rather than not to lose, and as a result you see more creativity, more leadership, more innovation."[1]

William Fuller, Human Resources Director—Bank of Boston Corporation

F ew would argue that the ability to innovate is critical to marketplace success. To prosper in today's ever-changing world, organizations must constantly introduce new products and services in response to changing customer needs. In the words of Peter Drucker, "Entrepreneurship rests on a theory of economy and society. The theory sees change as normal and indeed as healthy. And it sees the major task in society—and especially in the economy—as doing something different rather than doing better what is already being done."[2]

The ability to innovate is equally critical to the successful management of human resources. While many institutions to-day are still attempting to manage employee diversity through the restrictive method of assimilation, a number of progressive organizations are at the forefront in their efforts to value, not repress, diversity as a competitive resource. Rather than follow the old rules, they are rewriting many in response to today's workforce realities. While these leading-edge organizations are in the process of defining the standards of the future, most of their counterparts are still mired in the assumptions and practices of the past.

Based on what is now known about organization cultures that value assimilation, what might one expect to see done *differently* in those that value diversity? In this chapter, the distinct characteristics, assumptions, and practices commonly found in these organizations will be reviewed. In addition, their impact on employees will also be examined.

In an effort to identify commonalities, the authors investigated a variety of programs, revised practices, and other "valuing diversity" initiatives under way in public and private organizations throughout the United States. In particular, this investigation focused on 50 organizations considered to be leading edge in their efforts to institutionalize the value of employee diversity. The list included many private sector organizations as well as some public, labor, and academic institutions from all major geographic areas within the United States.

For the purpose of the survey, **leading-edge organizations** were defined as **those with a declared commitment to the value of diversity that are actively engaged in a variety of efforts aimed at institutionalizing this philosophy.** Based on a careful review of change efforts in progress within these 50 institutions, the authors identified a number of characteristics and practices shared by many leading-edge organizations. These commonalities will be discussed at length in this chapter.

As we begin this exploration, it should be noted that *none* of the institutions included in this survey have finished creating cultures of diversity. On the contrary, in most of these organizations, managers and employees recognize that the task of culture change has only just begun. Nonetheless, change *is* occurring and sustained evidence suggests that it will continue to build momentum. While common ground is not yet a reality, it is a future goal. Hence, these institutions are among those at the leading edge of efforts to value diversity and manage it as a vital resource.

COMMON CHARACTERISTICS IN
LEADING-EDGE ORGANIZATIONS

Because *different* issues have stimulated interest in valuing diversity within organizations, the programs and policies being developed to respond to the issues can vary significantly. Nonetheless, in looking across leading-edge organizations, there appear to be three shared characteristics. These include:

• Support and involvement of senior managers.

• "Different but equal" operating philosophy.

• Expanded definitions of effective performance.

Support and Involvement of Senior Managers

Because valuing diversity represents a major change in the management of human resources, it cannot succeed without endorsement at all levels. Within leading-edge institutions, this realization has mobilized senior executives to become visibly and philosophically identified with efforts to promote a culture of diversity. These executives seek additional knowledge about the issues, speak the language of diversity, and attempt to "walk the talk" as they set policy and provide guidance. Rather than position themselves as experts, senior managers tend to present themselves as motivated learners with a personal and professional interest in acquiring greater knowledge.

For example, at Levi Strauss & Company, the world's largest apparel manufacturer, senior executives not only participate in a 3-day workshop on "valuing diversity," they also serve as faculty for the classes that are open to all managers. In addition, as part of a long-term strategy aimed at changing the corporate culture, many executives participate in team building sessions and other activities designed to encourage open dialogue among employees about diversity issues and opportunities in the company.

In many leading-edge organizations, executive support is not only apparent to managers and employees, it is also evident to external stakeholders including customers, shareholders, local communities, and suppliers. As such, those outside the organization recognize that diversity is a fundamental value that will not be compromised or sacrificed to achieve profit or productivity goals.

When external events challenge the organization's commitment to diversity, senior managers are prepared to act in ways consistent with this value. For example, in 1987, U S West, Inc., a regional telecommunications company headquartered in Denver and widely known for its support for the value of diversity, was confronted with complaints about sexist and racist actions taken by one of its advertising agencies. After investigating these customer complaints, the company decided to pull its $10 million account from the agency, citing its "commitment to pluralism" as the primary reason for this sudden change.[3]

Different but Equal Operating Philosophy

In most leading-edge organizations, managers recognize the important difference between equal treatment and the same treatment. They do not judge all employees by the standard of the homogeneous ideal. Instead, managers respect the varied perspectives and communication styles of diverse employees. In evaluating performance, effort is made to distinguish style from substance—so that many styles and approaches can be accommodated without sacrificing effectiveness within the organization.

As understanding of the value of diversity grows throughout leading-edge organizations, the distinction between equality and sameness becomes clearer. Employees recognize that many styles exist and can be effective within a work group. They see the benefit of tapping diverse styles in their own creative output. Instead of ignoring core differences, employees recognize **others** and grow to respect them as equal contributors.

Expanded Definitions of Effective Performance

As the homogeneous ideal fades and becomes history, new standards of effective performance will inevitably be required. In many leading-edge organizations, these standards are now being developed by diverse employee groups who understand the organization's needs and also recognize the untapped talent that those outside the mainstream can offer.

As leading-edge organizations become more aware of the influence that cultural bias and the homogeneous ideal have had on past performance standards, many are beginning to question the relevance of traditional performance measures of management skill. One procedure that has come under increasing scrutiny is the formal management assessment process that many large organizations use to identify employees with advancement potential. In response to growing concern from diverse employees, these organizations are recognizing how formal assessment standards and methods can support the status quo and undermine the confidence and competencies of **others.**

For example, at a leading consumer products company in the Northeast, the management assessment process, used to identify employees with high potential, has recently come under criticism for alleged gender bias. According to a spokesperson for the women employees' network, the group that recently lodged a formal complaint with senior management, "Our company's assessment process rewards competitive and combative behavior at the expense of cooperative behavior. Because most men are trained to be competitive, they tend to do well in assessment. Women who go through the process are often criticized for being 'too supportive' in the group problem-solving exercises. Many have been told that they need to change their approach, take charge more and get tougher. . . .

"Because they use a softer, more supportive approach, a lot of excellent women managers get poor evaluations in assessment. They're great managers in the office. People love to work for them but they get poor evaluations when they're assessed. We believe this is happening because the entire process is culturally biased. We also believe it should be changed."

To help reduce the cultural bias that is built into many assessment center programs, institutions are now providing in-depth awareness training about stereotyping and cultural differences for all assessors. However, even with additional training for assessors, the question of relevance of formal assessment procedures continues to be discussed and debated. Leading-edge organizations realize that many of these assess-

ment tools need to be modified to reflect the diverse communication styles of the multicultural workforce. Until then, they
are likely to work against the value of employee diversity and
reinforce the status quo.

COMMON ORGANIZATIONAL ASSUMPTIONS

Once diversity is accepted as an organizational value, a new set
of assumptions about **otherness** begins to operate within the
institution. These assumptions are based on the positive contributions that diversity is perceived to offer. They are generally
accepted by managers and employees and, while they may not
be written down or well articulated, these assumptions influence the day-to-day actions of the organization and the behavior of employees. Within leading-edge organizations, three assumptions appear to be widely accepted. A discussion of each
assumption follows.

Assumption 1: Employee Diversity Is a Competitive Advantage

Within leading-edge organizations, there is little debate about
the importance of valuing diversity or the need for change. Instead, most managers and employees understand that diversity is a current reality. They also assume it can become an
important competitive advantage in the workplace and the
marketplace if it is valued and supported.

Rather than treat employee diversity as a growing threat or
problem, leading-edge organizations see it as a means of enhancing their recruitment, marketing, and customer service efforts. As one corporate recruiter stated, "If we succeed in creating a culture of diversity, we'll be able to prevail over our
competitors in campus recruiting. Women and minorities will
know about us. They will recognize there is more opportunity
in a culture that values their diversity."

Assumption 2: The Organization Is in Transition

As awareness builds and the culture evolves in leading-edge
organizations, managers become more able to recognize areas
in need of change while **others** become less impatient with the

pace of culture change. Regardless of differences in core identity, employees come to recognize that establishing common ground and creating a culture of diversity are long-term goals. They understand that both require ongoing discussion, debate, and modification—over several years.

Even in the few institutions that have been engaged in planned culture change for 5 to 10 years, managers and employees continue to talk of these organizations as being in transition. While they are getting closer to the goals of common ground and a culture of diversity, these institutions are still uncovering traditions, practices, and embedded biases that continue to advantage mainstream employees over **others.** Although these cultures have become more accepting and supportive of diversity, powerful vestiges of the old order still remain. Hence, employees at all levels continue to work for change and strive for improvement.

Assumption 3: Change the Culture, Not the People

Undoubtedly, the most common assumption within leading-edge organizations today is the belief that valuing diversity requires the organization culture to change and *not* the people. Unlike institutions that still attempt to retrain, coach, counsel, and cajole **others** to "fit" within the mainstream, leading-edge organizations focus on modifying policies and systems to support diversity. They are committed to retiring the homogeneous ideal in order to make room for core differences.

This focus on culture change rather than individual change often leads to different conclusions about the root cause of issues affecting **others.** Instead of blaming those individuals who cannot or will not adapt, the organization itself takes responsibility for the "poor chemistry" and views the work climate as a potential cause of problems. This shift in focus also helps managers see organizational patterns in the treatment of **others** that point to problems beyond individual performance.

As an example, within E. I. du Pont de Nemours & Co., Inc., several years of active recruitment of women and black engineers did little to change corporate demographics because early plateauing and turnover were unusually high among members of these groups.[4] Rather than assume **others** were to blame for their own lack of progress, one senior manager decided to look at the corporate environment to understand the root causes of this persistent problem. As this executive stated, "Blacks and women were leaving after a few years. Those that remained were not happy. Something was wrong. It was not a problem that could be solved with a slide rule."[5]

After a thorough examination of the issues, the environment itself was found to be a major cause of the problem. This discovery has since led to a series of planned efforts aimed at achieving cultural diversity at all levels. While it would have been less wrenching for Du Pont to focus on training **others** to modify their behavior in order to become more successful, this strategy would not have solved the problem. Within leading-edge organizations, solving the problem through culture change rather than by fixing **others** is what is seen as important.

COMMON ORGANIZATIONAL PRACTICES

As mentioned earlier, leading-edge organizations have many unique efforts under way to institutionalize the value of diversity. Each is developing its own, tailored plan. Nevertheless, there are common practices that distinguish these institutions from others. The way in which they are combined creates a variety of institutional approaches to change. As such, these common practices serve as the glue that holds the varied pieces of the institutional change effort together. They include:

- Diversity linked to strategic vision.
- Management responsibility for climate setting.
- Systems and procedures that support diversity.
- Ongoing monitoring of recruitment, promotion, and development trends.
- Organizational commitment to technical reeducation.
- Awareness education as an organizational priority.
- Rewards based on results.
- Enhanced benefits.

- Reinforcement of the value of diversity in hiring and promotions.
- Attention to subtle reinforcers of the homogeneous ideal.

Diversity Linked to Strategic Vision

One practice that distinguishes leading-edge organizations from others is the linkage made between diversity and the organization's long-range strategic vision. Within many corporations such as NYNEX Mobile Communications Company (NMCC), employee diversity is acknowledged to be of increasing strategic importance as globalization, market segmentation, and customer diversity increase. Utilizing the skills of a diverse workforce and managing diversity as a vital resource are seen as critical steps in corporate efforts to understand the changing marketplace and improve customer/client relations.

Within the academic community, leading-edge institutions are also working to link diversity and strategic vision. One well-publicized example is Stanford University, located on the Pacific Rim in Palo Alto, California. During the 1980s, Stanford drew strong criticism, particularly from many students of color, for its lack of attention to diversity. Since then, the university has revamped its undergraduate curriculum to reflect more of the teachings and ideas of diverse cultures and is now committed to building "an interactive, pluralistic community of students, faculty, and staff." To assist with the task of culture change, Stanford convenes an annual review panel composed of people from the campus and the surrounding community to assess yearly progress in achieving the long-term goal of multiculturalism. According to one senior administrator involved in this culture change effort, multiculturalism is now viewed by Stanford's faculty and staff as "both a moral and strategic imperative."[6]

Management Responsibility for Building a Supportive Work Climate

While most leading-edge organizations involve employees at all levels in efforts to change the culture, they also believe there is a special, ongoing role that managers must play as well. This role is **facilitator of change.** Because managers are responsible for coaching, developing, and empowering employees, they can play a critical role in supporting the value of diversity through their day-to-day efforts.

To be effective as facilitators, most managers need to develop a new set of skills. Since "taking charge" is often not the best way to achieve results through **others,** managers have to learn to redefine their roles. Instead of functioning as traditional supervisors, they need to empower and support **others.** Where they once made unilateral decisions, managers now need to develop the skills required to tap ideas and opinions within their work groups. Above all, they need to develop a multicultural perspective about the organization environment and learn to recognize how the culture impacts the performance and opportunities of **others.**

In organizations that value diversity, effective management is not defined in terms of controlling employee behavior and monitoring performance. Instead, it is the responsibility of every manager to create a motivating work climate that taps the talents of employees as it encourages cooperation and mutual respect. Within companies like Corning Glass Works, managers are evaluated based on their ability to "create a congenial environment" for diverse employees.[7] Both attrition and employee opinion survey results are used to assess the degree to which each manager succeeds in helping the organization support **others** and value diversity.

Systems and Procedures that Support Diversity

Unlike institutions that hire diverse employees but do nothing to change their internal cultures, leading-edge organizations recognize that their systems and procedures must evolve in order to maximize the contributions of **others.** As such, these institutions understand that enabling mechanisms that maximize the contributions of **others** are a vital component of efforts to manage diversity as an asset.

For example, within the Marriott Corporation, "supported employment" mechanisms have been developed to increase the probability of job success among differently abled employees. As such, job coaches are assigned to follow up with an emp...

Today, as a result o... su...

employs more than 6,000 differently a...
the initial training investment is considerable, the company believes it is well worth it. According to one manager involved in
the effort, "There is less turnover among disabled employees.
Once peak performance is achieved, it is usually maintained."

Organizations that value diversity also recognize they cannot afford to wait for federal hiring and antidiscrimination policies to catch up to the diversity that already exists in the workplace. As such, many have set nondiscriminatory policies that
go beyond federal guidelines to assure that employment rights
of **others** are protected. For example, in organizations like U S
West and Rolm Corporation, nondiscriminatory policies have
been developed to guarantee the employment rights of gay and
lesbian workers not protected under current federal employment legislation.[9]

Ongoing Monitoring of Recruitment, Promotion, and Development Trends

While most efforts to value diversity focus more on quality than
quantity, leading-edge organizations understand that hiring
and promotion statistics are important measures of ongoing
commitment to this change. Regardless of what is said about
diversity, the actual numbers of **others** at every level of the organization are often the most accurate measures of overall commitment. When these statistics reflect an ongoing increase in
employee diversity over time, organizations are indeed "walk-
ing the talk." When they do not, the lack of numerical progress
often indicates continued resistance to change.

In some cases, careful monitoring of hiring and promotion
activity leads to the identification of obstacles impeding the
progress of **others.** Often, these obstacles are attitudinal and
can be corrected with employee training. In other cases, they

may be procedural—requiring new systems or methods. In either situation, such obstacles are taken seriously and addressed immediately in institutions that value diversity.

For example, at Mobil Corporation, when women and people of color were unable to move beyond the glass ceiling of specialized middle management into executive positions in the $100,000 to $170,000 range, a procedural change was made to address the problem. First, a special committee of executives was convened to identify high-potential candidates. Then the committee was given responsibility for placing each candidate in a line management position viewed as "critical" for advancement into general management. Rather than restrict **others** to promotions within their particular disciplines, the company created this new procedure to provide diverse employees with the added visibility and mobility required to move up the executive ladder.[10]

Organizational Commitment to Technical Reeducation

As demand for skilled labor increases and supply decreases throughout the American workplace, some organizations are providing basic education to entry-level employees in order to upgrade their skills. While many organizations insist that basic education is "not the responsibility of employers," leading-edge institutions understand that the knowledge gap is growing in America—creating a shortage of qualified applicants for entry-level jobs and increasing the number of Americans deemed unemployable.

Rather than let this tragic situation continue to worsen, some organizations are taking remedial action now. In order to meet their own internal requirements for skilled workers, these companies are investing in basic education to help employees meet current and future job requirements. At Aetna Life and Casualty in Hartford, Connecticut, more than 1,000 workers have been hired through a cooperative educational effort with local organizations that focuses on reading and written communication skills.[11] Within the Marriott Corporation, a community employment and training department has been working in cooperative efforts with the U.S. government for the last 10 years to train and hire educationally disadvantaged people. The department, which has grown in size from 2 to 20, is responsible for preemployment training, counseling, and job placement of graduates.

Needless to say, organizations engaged in such efforts hope to see a payout in terms of improved productivity and reduced turnover. In the case of Aetna, the company hopes to see the payoff "in five to eight years from now."[12] At Marriott, turnover studies already indicate that employees who attend preemployment training and receive counseling on benefits, and so on, have a higher retention rate than those who do not.

Awareness Education as an Organizational Priority

While new programs and structures can do much to open doors and increase opportunity for **others,** these efforts must be guided by aware managers in order to ensure long-term success. Moreover, they must be supported by employees who are sensitive to diversity issues and able to resolve differences with **others** in a cooperative manner.

Despite assumptions to the contrary, awareness about **otherness** is not innate—it is learned. The learning process requires concentration, in-depth listening, personal reflection, and ongoing interaction with **others.** In organizations committed to valuing diversity, education is seen as a fundamental, critical step in efforts to change the culture. Because no one is an expert on employee diversity, leading-edge institutions rightly assume that everyone can benefit from awareness education.

Among the many institutions investing in training to prepare managers to work effectively with **others,** Honeywell, Inc., is at the forefront. Over the past several years, it has provided awareness education that "emphasizes the importance of understanding and valuing differences" to more than 85 percent of its managers.[13] Within U S West, employees at all levels are included in diversity training. Currently, the company offers two programs to its more than 70,000 employees: a one-day awareness workshop that explores the impact of culture, stereotyping, and collusion in the workplace, and a three-day seminar that examines the relationship between employee diversity and effective leadership.

Developed in collaboration with two organization consultants, Dr. Thomas A. Gordon of Philadelphia and Marilyn Loden, one of the authors of this book, these programs have become prototypes for similar training efforts in organizations across the United States. Within U S West, the workshops continue to be the cornerstone in corporate educational efforts aimed at replacing destructive "isms" with a far more positive one: pluralism.

In addition to general awareness training for all employees, many organizations also provide career development and empowerment seminars for diverse employees. Such programs are often designed to address the specific career concerns and developmental needs of women and people of color. While many organizations refer to training for employees with a shared core identity as "empowerment" or "efficacy seminars," it appears that some programs are more efficacious than others. Where programs reinforce the value of workforce diversity, they often help employees build support networks, solve some individual performance problems, identify critical organizational issues, and, occasionally, provide feedback to the institution. What efficacy seminars cannot do is change the mainstream culture.

In organizations with less commitment to the value of diversity, efficacy training for **others** is becoming quite popular. Employees who attend training sometimes describe it as providing "tactics to manipulate the system." The underlying assumption seems to be that the system itself will never change. To the degree that efficacy training shifts the need for change from the organization to **others,** it reinforces assimilation as a self-management strategy. Such training also sends a clear message to employees about working the system for survival rather than changing the system and establishing common ground.

In organizations like Du Pont, Apple Computers, and Philip Morris, U.S.A., career development or efficacy seminars are offered for women, people of color, and other diverse groups as part of a larger curriculum emphasizing the value of employee diversity. Participants are encouraged to share common experiences and concerns and to become resources to each other. However, the "blame the victim" and "us against the system" themes, popular in some empowerment and efficacy training efforts, are not stressed—since employees recognize they are also part of a systemwide effort to create a culture of diversity.

Rewards Based on Results

As institutions become aware of the powerful influence that assimilation has on performance standards, some are beginning to recognize how this influence can inhibit the performance of **others.** Typically, assimilation leads to homogenized standards that support the personal and managerial styles of those in the dominant group over the styles of **others.** By shifting the focus away from style to performance results, many leading-edge organizations are enlarging the range of acceptable behavior for diverse employees while remaining focused on quality performance.

For example, in a recent article appearing in *The GAO Journal*, Ira Goldstein, assistant comptroller general for operations at the U.S. General Accounting Office, commented on the increasing importance of rewards for performance within the public sector. In it, he stated:

> As one looks to the future, it becomes clear that human resource management skills will become simultaneously more essential and more difficult to apply. . . . Supervisors will increasingly face the challenge of relating to staff from diverse backgrounds. People from differing backgrounds often communicate, behave, and respond differently. As managers and supervisors, we must be able to accept differences in style, focusing instead on the results achieved. The ability to do this will be essential to getting the job done well.[14]

Enhanced Benefits

Along with efforts to improve work relationships and the climate in the workplace, institutions that value diversity are also busy revamping their benefit plans to respond to the increasingly diverse needs of employees. In addition to support for child care, some leading-edge institutions are now responding to the equally critical need for elder care that exists throughout America today.

Within International Business Machines Corporation (IBM), rated "Best in Benefits" in a study conducted by *The Wall Street Journal*, a child-care consultation service has provided more than 21,000 IBM families with information about local day-care options in 200 communities across the country. In addition, the company offers a similar service to employees responsible for elder care. A company-funded network of agencies provides consultation on medical services, home delivered meals, and other related services. Other IBM benefits include flexible work schedules, financial support for family adoption, subsidization of job searches for spouses whose careers are disrupted by company relocations, and part-time employment for individuals returning to work after extended unpaid leaves.[15]

Of the many benefits still on the "wish lists" of employees in the American workplace, none can be higher in importance than quality day care. While some companies are following IBM's lead and offering consultation services to help employees find local providers or subsidizing the training of local day-care providers to meet employee demand, relatively few are choosing to provide this service directly. Yet, most organizations that provide on-site day care point to improved productivity, reduced absenteeism, and enhanced worker morale as direct results.[16]

In the future, as competition increases for skilled employees, on-site day care is likely to be a deciding factor in many personal employment decisions. Therefore, what organizations decide to do about this issue *now* will have a direct bearing on their ability to compete successfully for talented employees in the future. Hopefully, as more institutions discover creative ways to meet the demand for on-site day care, fewer will choose to use legal liability as an excuse for avoiding this critical issue.

Reinforcement of the Value of Diversity in Hiring and Promotions

Looking back at our EEO history, one cannot help but notice the raging controversy that has occurred in many organizations regarding hiring and performance standards. With the advent of affirmative action programs in the early 1970s, "preserving standards" and "maintaining quality" became shorthand for keeping **others** out. Even today, the controversy over standards continues in many organizations that support the homogeneous ideal. This controversy is largely the result of unresolved conflicts over whose standards to apply: the dominant group's or different standards entirely.

While the need for high performance standards is incontestable, leading-edge organizations recognize the need for standards that accommodate a variety of personal styles. These organizations see the fallacy in the old argument that diversity lowers standards. Based on their accumulated experience, they know that diversity can lead to improved performance. As such, increased diversity is seen as a desirable goal *in and of itself*. It is vigorously pursued in hiring and promotion activities, rather than avoided or minimized.

In organizations like Digital Equipment Corporation, seeking out diverse employees has become a major focus of company recruiting efforts. Because DEC expects women and people of color to account for more than 50 percent of its workforce by the year 2000, the company is working now to strengthen its ties to professional societies and associations that can help identify **others** as future candidates for employment.[17]

Attention to Subtle Reinforcers of the Homogeneous Ideal

Among the many practices common within leading-edge organizations, none is more subtle yet powerful than the attention paid to language and customs that reinforce the homogeneous ideal. In leading-edge organizations, employees recognize the need to modify corporate language out of respect for diversity. Therefore, terms like *minority* are replaced in written and oral communciations with less loaded, more appropriate and inclusive phrases like African-American, Asian-American, American Indian, and person of color.

In addition, in leading-edge organizations, careful thought is now given to the variety of incentives offered to diverse employees as rewards for performance. For example, instead of assuming that all sales employees want tickets to sporting events as a reward for increased sales, a variety of choices is now offered such as dinner for two or tickets to a local concert. Rather than organize company outings around competitive team sports, a variety of activities is planned—including the option of nonparticipation. Instead of assuming that every employee will bring a spouse to social gatherings, institutions are starting to recognize that many may bring significant **others,** domestic partners, or choose to attend alone.

Each of these changes represents a subtle but important shift away from the culture of homogeneity. Each signals employees that diversity is recognized and valued. While some may say such attention to detail is unnecessary, employees often measure their organization's true commitment to the value of diversity by examining the subtle ways in which it is supported or ignored. Hence, these small shifts in emphasis often carry considerable weight with **others.**

ORGANIZATIONAL IMPACT ON ALL EMPLOYEES

Taken together, the common practices discussed in this chapter and found in many leading-edge institutions are beginning to exert a noticeable impact on some organizational cultures. Together, they are diminishing the importance of assimilation and the pursuit of the homogeneous ideal and increasing the emphasis placed on valuing diversity and establishing common ground. While no single practice can create a culture of diversity, there is synergy developing in institutions where many of these practices are operative. This synergy is leading to:

- The increased presence of **others** in visible leadership roles.

- A stronger voice for **others** in culture change efforts.

- The emergence of integrated employee networks.

Increased Presence of Others in Visible Leadership Roles

While the emphasis placed on organizational practices discussed in this chapter is often a measure of commitment to change, the best long-term measure of institutional commitment is still quantitative. When all is said and done, the movement of **others** into visible leadership roles is the most direct measure of institutional support for the value of diversity. How are leading-edge organizations doing here? While there is certainly room for improvement in virtually every case, the glass ceiling that has prevented **others** from rising to the top is beginning to crack in some institutions. In addition, **others** are also entering technical fields where, historically, their numbers have been extremely scarce.

Since the passage of the Civil Rights Act of 1964, it has been legally possible for **others** to take their rightful places at the helm of organizations—but rights do not automatically translate into reality. Events of the past two decades have proven that the increased presence of **others** at the top is not a natural, evolutionary process. It is a change that takes planning, proaction, monitoring, and follow-up. While the practices discussed in this chapter can increase support for this change, specific goals and timetables for hiring and promotion are also required. Neither the practices discussed in this chapter nor goals and timetables alone are as effective as they are together. Combined, these common practices and targeted goals offer organizations the best chance of changing attitudes and behaviors while achieving true integration at all levels and in all job categories.

Stronger Voice for Others in Culture Change Efforts

As the various practices discussed in this chapter change the organizational mind-set from homogeneity to the value of diversity, another noticeable impact occurs. Those formerly thought to be outside the mainstream become important resources in the culture change process. Their ideas are solicited by those in the dominant group. Their experiences as **others** on the periphery of the mainstream culture are acknowledged and become important benchmarks for change.

In many organizations, including Xerox Corporation, U S West, and Avon, employee resource groups have become an important source of feedback for senior management.[18] Often created by employees themselves, these networks help senior management understand how policies, practices, and the mainstream culture affect **others.** Composed largely of employees who share a particular core identity, resource groups usually have unrestricted access to members of senior management. Most meet on a regular basis with organizational leaders to discuss issues and offer suggestions aimed at enhancing the work environment and improving work relationships. In leading-edge organizations, feedback from **others** is not just solicited through employee networks and resource groups. It is also acted on.

Emergence of Integrated Networks

Single-issue resource groups that raise the organization's consciousness about race, gender, sexual/affectional orientation, and so on, have helped influence hiring and promotion activities, policy formation, and employee benefits planning in many leading-edge institutions. Typically, such networks focus on the special concerns and interests of a subset of **others**. They are less concerned with the impact of organizational policies and practices on *all* employees. However, as the cultures of leading-edge institutions evolve, the need for integrated networks that can move beyond the role of resource groups is becoming more apparent. Today, in a few institutions that have been involved in culture change for several years, integrated networks are beginning to emerge. By leveraging off the special interests and unique perspectives of resource groups, these diverse networks are turning their attention and energies to the establishment of common ground. Rather than replace single-issue resource groups, they are working to establish cooperative alliances among employees of all core identities. These groups represent an important step forward for leading-edge organizations. They are employee networks that both value differences and see true integration as the ultimate goal. In essence, they are the true expression of the value of diversity and the organization's hope for a better, more productive future.

NOTES

1. Lennie Copeland, "Making the Most of Cultural Differences at the Workplace," *Personnel*, June 1988, p. 56.
2. Peter F. Drucker, *Innovation and Entrepreneurship* (New York: Harper & Row, 1985), p. 26.

3. Betty Lehan Harragan, "The $10 Million Blunder," *Working Woman*, May 1988, p. 97.
4. David Maraniss, "Firm Makes Racial Revolution from Top Down," *The Washington Post*, March 8, 1990, p. A1.
5. Ibid., p. A22.
6. Stanford University Self-Study on Building a Multiracial Multicultural University Community, Stanford University, April 1990, pp. 1–4.
7. Peggy Schmidt, "Women and Minorities: Is Industry Ready?" *New York Times*, October 16, 1988, p. 25.
8. Peter T. Kilborn, "For the Retarded, Independence in Real Jobs," *New York Times*, January 2, 1990, p. 1.
9. Dianna Solis, "Gays Band Together in Workplace to Help Careers, Battle Prejudice," *The Wall Street Journal*, March 12, 1986, p. B1.
10. "How Companies Help," *Nation's Business*, May 1987, p. 27.
11. Amanda Bennett, "As Pool of Skilled Help Tightens, Firms Move to Broaden Their Role," *The Wall Street Journal*, May 8, 1989, p. 1.
12. Ibid.
13. Schmidt, "Women and Minorities: Is Industry Ready?" p. 25.
14. Ira Goldstein, "Managing for Performance in the Public Sector," *The GAO Journal*, no. 7 (Fall 1989), p. 51.
15. Cathy Trost, "Best Employers for Women and Parents," *The Wall Street Journal*, November 30, 1987, p. 21.
16. Kathy Rebello, "It May Be the Benefit of the '90's," *USA Today*, September 21, 1988, p. B–1.
17. Bennett, "As Pool Tightens, Firms Broaden Role," p. A4.
18. Marcus Mabry, "Past Tokenism," *Newsweek*, May 14, 1990, p. 38.

Chapter Ten

The Pluralistic Leader

"Like portfolios, organizations benefit from diversity. Effective leaders resist the urge to people their staffs only with others who look or sound or think just like themselves. . . . They look for good people from many molds, and then they encourage them to speak out, even to disagree."[1]

Warren G. Bennis,
Distinguished Professor of Business Administration—USC

W ithin most organizations in America, valuing employee diversity begins as a grass roots movement. It often starts as a constructive reaction to limits imposed on **others** by the mainstream culture. Even when the value of diversity is acknowledged by those at the top of organizations, it is usually after the fact. Long before leaders at the top recognize what **others** offer the organization, this added value is being demonstrated, recognized, *and* repressed at lower levels. In general, both the opportunities and the barriers associated with managing employee diversity as a vital resource are apparent to employees at the bottom and the middle before they become apparent to those at the top.

This fact of institutional life challenges many assumptions

made about the role and function of leaders. In particular, it is in opposition to the traditional belief that organizational leaders are the repository of all knowledge and, usually, the first to know. In reality, when it comes to understanding and valuing diversity, organizational leaders are often among the last to know. When they do become aware of diversity, they seldom have a clear picture of how to respond. For while thousands of seminars, articles, and books have been written about effective leadership for the American workplace, none has directly addressed the challenges posed by employee diversity and the skills required to lead **others** effectively.

PARTICIPATIVE VERSUS PLURALISTIC LEADERSHIP

Yet, new attitudes and skills are clearly required to lead diverse organizations and manage **others** as a vital resource. Within organizations that value diversity, effective **managers** are those with the skills required to **empower** diverse employees. Effective **leaders** must go beyond these basic competencies. They must also be able to **inspire** employees to act in support of organizational goals. To provide inspiration, leaders need to be visibly committed to the creation of a culture of diversity. They must maintain high credibility with **others** by moving beyond current models of participative leadership to become **pluralistic leaders.**

Until now, participative leadership has been the model used to guide the behavior of leaders and managers in most successful U.S. organizations. This model is based on the assumption that something valuable can be learned from employees. It emphasizes empowerment and increased employee involvement in problem solving. **Pluralistic leadership goes beyond participative leadership.** While it also emphasizes empowerment and employee involvement, it assumes that the organization culture needs to change if diversity is to become a true asset. This culture change must be a collaborative process involving **others** as well as those in the mainstream. At the center of this change is the leader—inspiring commitment among **others** through personal and organizational proaction.

PLURALISTIC LEADERSHIP CHARACTERISTICS

In 1989, in an effort to isolate specific dimensions of pluralistic leadership, one of the authors of this book, Marilyn Loden, together with another consultant, Dr. Thomas A. Gordon, sought input from a diverse cross section of employees in public, private, and academic institutions. Based on their collective experience consulting to organizations, both consultants believed pluralistic leadership qualities were often more apparent to **others** than to those in the mainstream. Therefore, their research included interviews with employees at every level of organizations—from the shop floor to the executive suite. After analyzing input from over 200 individuals in 20 public and private institutions, a model of pluralistic leadership began to emerge. Based on initial research results, five dimensions were identified as key components of effective pluralistic leadership. To further refine this model, a survey was then developed and administered to 450 employees.[2] Participants included managers and employees from a diverse group of public, private, academic, and not-for-profit organizations. Respondents were asked to indicate the degree of importance that they ascribed to each leadership dimension identified in the model. They were also asked to identify any additional qualities that they believed were essential for effective pluralistic leadership. As a result of survey feedback, the model evolved to include six dimensions essential for effective leadership in diverse organizations. These dimensions include:

- Vision and values that recognize and support diversity within the organization.

- Ethical commitment to fairness and the elimination of all types of workplace discrimination.

- Broad knowledge and awareness regarding the primary and secondary dimensions of diversity and multicultural issues.

- Openness to change based on diverse input and feedback about personal filters and blind spots.

- Mentor and empowerer of diverse employees.

- Ongoing catalyst and model for individual and organizational change.

These six leadership dimensions consist of attitudes and roles that make leaders effective in organizations where diversity is valued. The first four relate primarily to the leader's values and attitudes. The last two describe specific roles that diverse employees believe must be played by effective leaders. In some cases, those surveyed cited specific examples of pluralistic leadership in action—drawing on their own work experiences and naming specific individuals within their organizations. In other cases, employees pointed out that, while they believed the six dimensions were important, they could find little evidence of them in action within their own organizations. Generally, employees believed this was due to the fact that pluralistic leadership was not valued within the organization culture.

What follows is a detailed report of the results of this leadership study. It includes a summary of the specific comments made by those surveyed and describes the principal attributes that define each leadership dimension. By reviewing this detailed description of pluralistic leadership attributes, managers and other leaders can gain insights into how they themselves can become more effective pluralistic leaders.

Organization Vision and Values that Recognize and Support Diversity

Throughout the ages, most leaders believed that predicting and controlling the future was something only the gods could do. Today, as a result of 20th-century advances in technology and various fields of intellectual endeavor, most U.S. leaders believe many powerful forces that will influence the future of their organizations can be anticipated and managed. Increased diversity in the workplace and the marketplace is certainly one of these forces. According to the vast majority of employees surveyed, pluralistic leaders are those who recognize the long-term importance of diversity.

In particular, participants believe that pluralistic leaders possess the values and the long-range vision required to maximize the benefits of employee diversity. This dimension was rated very highly by most employees. While leaders of organizations that value homogeneity minimize the long-range implications of an increasingly diverse workforce, pluralistic leaders do not. They understand that the importance of diversity will continue to increase in the future, necessitating careful planning now. As such, they see diversity as a key factor in all strategic planning efforts. As organization strategy is set, the long-term implications of increased diversity are duly noted and factored into the strategic mix.

Respondents also stated that pluralistic leaders are able to articulate the long-term benefits that diversity offers the American workplace and the larger society. These leaders recognize the enormous potential for growth and renewal present in the diverse perspectives of **others.** In order to tap this potential, they take affirmative steps to diversify their organizations, believing that the broader the spectrum of backgrounds, the richer the ideas that can potentially emerge.

One leader who holds this point of view is Nancy Woodhull, president of Gannett News Media. According to her account, *USA Today's* successful launching a decade ago was largely because of the organization's diversity. As she states, "Without women, *USA Today* would have been *USA Yesterday.* The reason we were interesting is that there were a lot of ideas from different people with different points of view in our news meetings every day. There were women; there were minorities, there were young people; there were old people. There were people who went to Harvard. There were people who went to Trenton State in New Jersey."[3]

Survey respondents also believe that pluralistic leaders see the interdependence that exists among diverse members of their organizations. They understand the importance of fostering cooperation and mutual respect at all levels and in all departments. As they plan for and anticipate future events, these leaders solicit ideas and opinions from **others.** Regardless of differences in style, perspective, and cultural heritage, they value the contributions of **others** and draw on the input of highly diverse sources in both planning and decision making. Respect for the views of **others** is an attribute that survey participants believe is highly important for effective leadership.

Participants also agreed that pluralistic leaders use the physical environment to reinforce their vision and the value of differences. As such, their use of space and decor highlights diversity as a valued norm in the organization. Because they understand the power of ritual, ceremony, and tradition in supporting the organization's core values, effective pluralistic leaders use these mechanisms to further efforts aimed at creating a culture of diversity.

So much has been written about the need for visionary leadership in the American workplace, one might think the topic would be exhausted by now. However, according to most employees interviewed, the majority of leaders in the American workplace still lack the vision and values required to support diversity long term. Regardless of their interest in the future, employees believe many leaders underestimate the long-term impact that diversity will have. In contrast to the majority, respondents think pluralistic leaders not only recognize this new reality, they view the growing impact of diversity as an opportunity and are preparing now to capitalize on it.

In organizations like Corning Glass Works, where Chairman James R. Houghton is an outspoken advocate for change, increasing the presence of women and people of color in middle and upper management is seen as a critical step in corporate efforts to capitalize on diversity. Four years ago, under Mr. Houghton's direction, the organization set challenging advancement goals to increase diversity at executive levels. So far, Corning has succeeded in meeting these self-imposed targets, and its retention of women and black employees has also improved significantly.[4]

Ethical Commitment to Fairness and the Elimination of "Isms"

Throughout the decade of the 80s, when the emphasis on money and status reached new heights within our society, organizational leaders were seldom singled out or applauded for their ethics. Instead, many leaders in both the public and private sectors were praised for being fiercely competitive, aggressive, ruthless, and bottom-line driven. While these may have been among the most admired leadership qualities in the White

House and on Wall Street a decade ago, today there is growing recognition of the need for a more balanced, ethical approach. The enormous human costs associated with decisions made by leaders who lacked ethics and heart have become increasingly apparent in the 1990s. By most objective accounts, deregulation, leveraged buyouts, insider trading, and merger mania have all taken a severe toll on many institutions and millions of American workers.

As a result of recent, traumatic events in the workplace, many employees surveyed appear to be convinced of the importance of ethical leadership for the 1990s and beyond. When it comes to valuing diversity, they believe an ethical commitment to fairness is a prerequisite for strong pluralistic leadership. According to more than 90 percent of those surveyed, leaders need to "walk the talk" of diversity to maintain credibility with **others.** In addition, many participants agreed that the leader's personal commitment to diversity must be based on both economic and moral considerations. As such, their actions must reflect a strong belief in the value of diversity as a practical business decision *and* a moral imperative.

Faced with difficult problems, employees maintain that pluralistic leaders will find solutions that do not force the organization to sacrifice the needs of employees for improved productivity. Because they understand that fair treatment and improved productivity are interdependent elements, pluralistic leaders seek solutions and create opportunities that reinforce the importance of both. In making decisions, they place ethical considerations regarding fairness, honesty, and equality before economic ones, believing that the best decisions for the organization are those that respect the rights of employees as they improve productivity and increase profitability.

Many employees also believe that pluralistic leaders understand the destructive impact of institutional "isms" on society. As such, they are committed to eliminating ageism, ethnocentrism, heterosexism, racism, sexism, and other forms of social discrimination from the workplace. Because most leaders possess the position power required to shape policies and practices, they can play a special role in eliminating workplace discrimination. This role is as a visible spokesperson for change. It is a role that employees believe pluralistic leaders are willing and able to fulfill.

According to those surveyed, pluralistic leaders must be prepared to speak out on issues of workplace discrimination— even at the risk of criticism from mainstream colleagues. This was true in 1990, when Michael Lee, president of the San Francisco Bar Association, challenged local law firms to improve their records of hiring and promoting people of color. Despite the potential risk of criticism from other attorneys, Lee was an outspoken critic of the past performance of many firms. Recognizing the platform he had for raising awareness, he also stated that he intended to use his post as top spokesperson for organized lawyers in San Francisco to fight discrimination.[5]

Broad Knowledge of Dimensions of Diversity and Awareness of Multicultural Issues

Of the six dimensions included in the model, none was thought to be of more importance for effective pluralistic leadership than broad knowledge of the dimensions of diversity and awareness of multicultural issues. Employees felt strongly that leaders of **others** cannot be effective without fundamental knowledge of **otherness.** While participants acknowledged that no one can be an expert on all the primary and secondary dimensions of diversity, they strongly agreed that leaders require basic knowledge of the six core dimensions of diversity including age, ethnicity, gender, physical ability/qualities, race, and sexual/affectional orientation. In addition, employees stated that effective pluralistic leadership also requires an in-depth understanding of issues such as culture clash, cultural myopia, garbled communication, the inherent limitations of assimilation as a strategy for managing **others,** and so on.

When it comes to developing awareness, many employees surveyed also believe that pluralistic leaders do not wait for **others** to come forward to educate them about the issues. Instead, these leaders seek out information about all the dimensions of diversity from a variety of sources. They keep current on issues related to employee diversity through discussions with **others,** readings, films, and so on. As their knowledge

base expands, pluralistic leaders also see the causal relationships that exist between global events, national events, community events, and diversity issues in the workplace.

Survey participants also agreed that language and communication skills are often the most obvious measures of a leader's
understanding of diversity issues. When leaders use inclusive
language, quote diverse sources, and readily adapt to differences in the communication styles of **others,** they display a
high level of respect for **otherness** and awareness of many diversity issues. When they use language that excludes or de-
values **others,** they reinforce stereotypes and appear to be unaware. In each case, employees indicated that the leader's
language is often a gauge of personal understanding and commitment to the value of diversity.

James E. Preston, president and chief operating officer of
Avon Products, Inc., is a leader of a diverse organization who
appreciates the subtleties of language. For example, while he
acknowledges that women can learn to speak "militarese" and
"sportspeak," he is not reluctant to ask the key question: "But
. . . why should they have to?"[6] Preston is also aware of the
importance of culture change to support diversity in the American workplace. Recognizing that most institutions have been
"described and imprinted by white males," he thinks it is not
surprising that **others** "have had difficulty over the years in
adapting to the climates that exist in these businesses."[7]

R. E. "Ted" Turner, chairman of the board and president of
Turner Broadcasting Systems, Inc., is also aware of the importance of language in all communications. As a business leader
with a strong interest in international relations, Turner believes
TBS employees should be sensitive to language usage. To reinforce the point that inclusive language can help to unify people
of diverse cultural backgrounds, he has instituted a corporate
practice whereby TBS employees can be fined up to $100 for
using the word *foreign* instead of the word *international* on company time.[8]

When it comes to heightened awareness, employees also believe that pluralistic leaders must be knowledgeable about *all*
core dimensions of difference—not just those they are familiar
with or comfortable exploring. Of the six core dimensions pre-

viously discussed, employees think most leaders have the lowest level of comfort and awareness dealing with differences in physical ability/qualities, and sexual/affectional orientation. As a result of this knowledge gap, many participants think differently abled, gay, and lesbian employees are less likely to advance to leadership positions within organizations.

A 1987 *Wall Street Journal* survey of 351 top executives supports this view regarding advancement for lesbians and gay men. According to the study, while only 1 percent of those surveyed would hesitate to promote a woman to management-committee level, 66 percent said they would hesitate to promote a gay employee to the same level.[9] These responses underscore the need for education and heightened awareness among leaders regarding issues related to sexual/affectional orientation. Although many mainstream executives have become increasingly comfortable with women as colleagues, these results indicate a continuing reluctance to accept gay employees in similar roles. As such, prejudice, homophobia, and heterosexism continue to be serious problems confronting gay men and lesbians in the American workplace.

Openness to Change

Another dimension of pluralistic leadership identified by the majority of employees surveyed was openness to feedback and to change. In particular, employees stated that pluralistic leaders appear to be more open to the diverse views and opinions of **others.** As evidence of this increased openness, they tend to include a more diverse mix of **others** in their personal and professional networks.

Because they are actively involved in expanding their own awareness, pluralistic leaders rely on their networks for information and diverse points of view. They encourage employees to challenge and disagree. They seem to value feedback from **others** about their personal behavior and blindspots. Rather than become defensive when their opinions or behavior are challenged, pluralistic leaders often appear more willing to modify their beliefs and actions—based on feedback from **others.**

This ability to accept feedback and modify behavior was rated as extremely important among those surveyed. In addition, the ability to empathize with **others** was also identified as an important quality that enhances trust and openness between organizational leaders and other employees. Within E. I. du Pont de Nemours & Co., Inc., where valuing diversity is strongly encouraged, Vice President Mark Suwyn stands out as an example of a mainstream leader who has demonstrated an openness to change. As a result of his experiences in awareness training, he believes he has become more conscious of his own blindspots.

As he stated, "I came to realize how I had been making decisions based on subconscious stereotypes. . . . I tended to favor human behavior like mine: aggressive, a little bit of the football player. When I said to myself, 'Who do I need for a tough job?'—I tended to look for a tough white man. Now I have a greater appreciation of what blacks had to do just to get here. From that I know they are prepared to do tough jobs."[10]

According to **others** at Du Pont, the change in this leader's attitude also led to proactive behavior in support of diversity. As one woman of color stated, "Mark Suwyn has changed tremendously. He took it on himself to ennoble and empower people. . . . Now I am valued in the organization. I wasn't before."[11] Such testimony provides strong evidence of the positive impact that leaders can have when they are willing to accept feedback from **others** and, in turn, reevaluate their own behavior.

Mentor and Empowerer of Diverse Employees

In discussing the specific roles and responsibilities of pluralistic leaders, employees stressed the importance of "mentoring" over all others. The majority of those surveyed characterized pluralistic leaders as those who are mentors or informal advisers to **others** as well as to employees of similar core identity. While there was a strong perception that most leaders in institutions act as informal mentors for some employees, respondents believed pluralistic leaders are more likely to reach out to diverse employees at many levels of the organization. As one employee wrote, "These leaders aren't interested in just cloning themselves. They want to see women and minorities make it, too."

One of the qualities that participants believe make pluralistic leaders more effective as mentors is their ability to give timely, constructive, and honest performance feedback. Among gays and people of color surveyed, this ability was thought to be particularly important for mainstream leaders. Some employees also drew a distinction between candid feedback and enlightened feedback; stating that "unaware leaders" may be very candid but also prejudiced in their assessment of the performance of **others**. Because they are usually viewed by **others** as more aware or enlightened, pluralistic leaders have less of a credibility problem when giving performance feedback. Even when the leader's feedback is critical, diverse employees stated they are more willing to accept or consider the criticism—without wondering if it is tainted by the leader's stereotypes and personal prejudices.

As mentors and empowerers, pluralistic leaders are perceived by employees to be more creative when it comes to spotlighting the talents of **others**. As such, they do not simply wait for opportunities to present themselves or operate through "normal channels." Pluralistic leaders seek out or create unique opportunities that actualize the potential of **others**. These opportunities take a variety of forms, from task force assignments and high-visibility presentations to new job opportunities that are created for talented **others**, not simply filled by them.

According to those surveyed, pluralistic leaders also employ and encourage managers to use a coaching style that is **enabling** rather than **controlling**. Because they believe in empowerment and maximizing the potential of all employees, these leaders recognize that managers in the organization must provide training, timely information, and ongoing support to assure employee success. As such, these leaders make a strong effort to reinforce and reward managers who empower employees and behave in ways that demonstrate respect for **others**.

Today, in organizations committed to valuing diversity, pluralistic leaders are working closely with diverse employees to increase communication, encourage employee participation, and solicit ideas and feedback that can help shape policies and practices. In companies such as Avon, Xerox, U S West, and Security Pacific Corporation, employee networks based on differences in race, gender, and so on are being encouraged. Not only do these groups provide **others** of similar core identities with ongoing support, they are also viewed as a valuable source of feedback by organizational leaders—some of whom serve as mentors and advisers to the various networks. As Robert Smith, president and CEO of Security Pacific stated, "Our multicultural networks provide us with the additional knowledge and understanding we need to develop shared values and common organizational goals."

Catalyst and Model for Personal and Organizational Change

Among those surveyed, there was virtually unanimous agreement that pluralistic leaders also play a critical role as catalysts for change within their organizations. Generally, they are credited by employees with "making culture change possible." According to employees, many of these leaders are also involved in efforts to increase understanding and respect for human diversity throughout society and internationally as well.

At the organizational level, pluralistic leaders use their power and influence to quicken the pace and increase the depth of culture change. While they recognize the importance of involving diverse employees in the change process, they are also personally involved in finding new systems, procedures, and solutions to problems that reinforce the value of diversity and utilize the talents of every employee. In this sense, they truly serve as *leaders* rather than observers or reluctant participants in the organization's efforts to value diversity.

At the personal level, pluralistic leaders also serve as role models for other individuals. According to those surveyed, this modeling takes several distinct forms. Sometimes, modeling occurs when these leaders talk about their own awareness development, sharing stories about their experiences with **others** and their efforts to manage personal stereotypes and prejudice.

Sometimes, modeling is done when they challenge colleagues about prejudices and stereotypes that delimit **others.** Often, pluralistic leaders serve as positive role models by simply displaying the day-to-day behaviors required to lead and inspire a diverse workforce.

According to the majority of those surveyed, pluralistic leaders are also skilled in resolving culture clash between diverse groups. By serving as third-party mediators, these leaders help conflicting parties understand the issues from the perspective of **others.** As they mediate disputes between **others,** pluralistic leaders reduce intergroup tensions and increase the probability that culture clash can become enhancing.

For example, nowhere is the leader's role as mediator more important than in a large, diverse, metropolitan community like the City of New York. Characterizing the diversity of New York as a "gorgeous mosaic," Mayor David N. Dinkins is a leader committed to increasing tolerance and respect among diverse groups. Since taking office in 1990, he has involved himself as a mediator in many disputes between **others,** stating in one case that he would "bear any burden, and walk any mile" to settle a clash between two racially diverse groups "through mediation and conciliation."[12]

As they go about the business of transforming the culture of organizations, pluralistic leaders recognize that they are engaged in far-reaching and important work. Although some may describe the movement from assimilation to valuing diversity as "revolutionary," to these leaders this change is natural, practical, and supportive of the fundamental goals and values of the institution.

As Edgar S. Woolard, Jr., chairman and CEO of Du Pont observed, "Other people hear what I'm saying and say, 'Listen, you're talking about a cultural revolution.' But I don't start out with that idea. My idea is just to use the enormous talent we have—all of it. To let blacks and women into the process, to give them a sense of belonging and power, to have biracial teams working together—all of that is important for our functioning as a company, and it can serve as a role model for the rest of America."[13]

PLURALISTIC LEADERSHIP AND OTHERS

Like the concept of valuing diversity, pluralistic leadership is also a grass roots model. It evolved out of the collective experiences, ideas, and perceptions of employees at all levels in many diverse organizations. As such, it is an amalgam of the values and opinions of both mainstream employees and **others.**

While this leadership model was shaped by diverse points of view and endorsed by those in and outside the mainstream, study results reveal that all six dimensions are viewed as more important by **others** as compared to white men. What's more, the degree of importance ascribed to each leadership dimension increases as core differences increase. Therefore, in terms of primary dimensions of diversity, those employees least like the dominant group in the American workplace view these pluralistic leadership dimensions as most important.

It is not surprising that employees with identities farthest removed from the homogeneous ideal are most sensitive to the attributes of effective pluralistic leadership. They are more aware of the importance of these qualities because they are more directly and negatively affected by their absence. Now, like finely calibrated barometers, they are alerting leaders to impending changes in the environment and pointing the way to a more productive future. To the extent that today's leaders can accept this input and adopt the pluralistic leadership model as their own, they will stand a far better chance of weathering the inevitable storms of change and succeeding in the future.

NOTES

1. Warren Bennis, "Followers Make Good Leaders Good," *New York Times*, December 31, 1989, p. B–2.
2. Thomas A. Gordon and Marilyn Loden, *Pluralistic Leadership Survey*, Copyright © 1989 by Loden Associates, Inc., and Interface Associates. All rights reserved.
3. Sharon Nelton, "Meet Your New Work Force," *Nation's Business*, July 1988, p. 15.
4. Carol Hymowitz, "One Firm's Bid to Keep Blacks, Women," *The Wall Street Journal*, February 16, 1989, p. 1.

5. Maitland Zane, "S.F. Bar Group Presses Minority Hiring," *San Francisco Chronicle*, March 5, 1990, p. B7.

6. Jolie Solomon, "Firms Address Workers' Cultural Variety," *The Wall Street Journal*, February 10, 1989, p. B1.

7. Nelton, "Meet Your New Work Force," p. 16.

8. "Harper's Index," *Harper's Magazine*, May 1990, p. 19.

9. Cynthia Crossen, "A Lingering Stigma," *The Wall Street Journal*, Special Report on Executive Style, March 20, 1987, p. 28D.

10. David Maraniss, "Firm Makes Racial Revolution from Top Down," *The Washington Post*, March 8, 1990, p. A22.

11. Ibid.

12. Todd S. Purdum, "Dinkins Asks for Racial Unity and Offers to Mediate Boycott," *New York Times*, May 12, 1990, p. 11.

13. Maraniss, "Firm Makes Racial Revolution," p. A22.

Chapter Eleven

Creating the Culture of Diversity

"*Unless we activate the human factor, that is, unless we take into consideration the diverse interests of people, work collectives, public bodies, and various social groups, unless we rely on them, and draw them into active, constructive endeavor, it will be impossible for us to accomplish any of the tasks set or to change the situation in this country.*"[1]

Mikhail Gorbachev, President—Union of Soviet Socialist Republics

E ach year, as diversity continues to grow within the American workplace, organizations are under increasing pressure to respond in a constructive rather than a reactive manner. To be ready for the workforce of the future, this constructive response must begin now. While leading-edge organizations provide valuable examples of what is being done to facilitate the change from assimilation to valuing differences, no single organization has created a true culture of diversity as yet. Nonetheless, early successes and failures of various valuing diversity efforts suggest that a basic blueprint for creating the culture of diversity does now exist.

By **culture of diversity,** we mean an **institutional environment built on the values of fairness, diversity, mutual respect, understanding, and cooperation; where shared goals, rewards, performance standards, operating norms, and a common vision of the future guide the efforts of every employee**

and manager. This culture is the ultimate goal of organizations seriously committed to the philosophy of valuing diversity.

The blueprint for creating the culture of diversity outlined in this chapter draws on the strengths of various leading-edge efforts *and goes beyond* what is currently being done. It describes initial, intermediate, and long-term actions necessary for successful institutional change. For employees, managers, and organizations committed to valuing differences, this blueprint outlines a comprehensive approach for creating the culture of diversity.

PHASE 1: SETTING THE STAGE

While the valuing diversity movement most often begins at the bottom in organizations, it must quickly involve those at the top—if it is to succeed long term. In particular, to assure that valuing diversity is seen as more than a "program" or "quick fix" solution, several initial actions must be taken by senior management and other organizational leaders to frame the overall effort. These early actions help create interest in the concept of valuing diversity by emphasizing the connection between diversity and the bottom line or improved organizational performance. They also set the stage for all programs and changes to follow.

To set the stage for culture change, organizational leaders must take an early, active, and visible role. In particular, their role must focus on:

- Acknowledging the fundamental difference between equal employment opportunity and valuing diversity.
- Endorsing the value of diversity and communicating this throughout the organization.
- Articulating a pluralistic vision.

EEO versus Valuing Diversity

One early question that must be anticipated by senior managers and other leaders as they set the stage for culture change is, "How is valuing diversity different from equal employment opportunity (EEO) and affirmative action (AA) programs?" In describing the distinctions between these efforts, it is important to emphasize that EEO and affirmative action have historically **focused on quantitative change.** In particular, EEO is a legalistic response to workplace discrimination originally mandated by the federal government. Affirmative action programs are outgrowths of equal employment law. Generally, they consist of specific hiring and promotion goals and timetables that are used to correct imbalances in the makeup of an organization's workforce resulting from long-term patterns of employment discrimination. While such programs have led to changes in the composition of the American workforce, they have not been tied to organizational culture change. Hence, many organizations in compliance with affirmative action goals and timetables continue to use the strategy of assimilation to manage increased employee diversity.

Valuing diversity builds on the foundation created by equal employment law and affirmative action efforts to hire and promote **others.** By focusing on **the quality of the work environment and improved utilization of the skills of** *all* **employees,** valuing diversity moves beyond affirmative action. It acknowledges that hiring and promoting diverse people does not automatically lead to mutual respect, cooperation, and true integration. To achieve these goals, organizations must also value the contributions of *all* employees and maximize their opportunities to contribute. Unlike EEO, valuing diversity is driven by the organizational need for increased innovation. It is a voluntary process that focuses on utilization of the skills of *all* employees.

The following list summarizes key differences between EEO/ AA programs and valuing diversity efforts:

EEO/Affirmative Action	*Valuing Diversity*
Government initiated	Voluntary
Legally driven	Productivity driven
Quantitative	Qualitative
Problem focused	Opportunity focused
Assumes assimilation	Assumes integration
Reactive	Proactive

When it comes to distinguishing between EEO/AA and valuing diversity, some people such as Alan Zimmerlee, manager of EEO/AA and Valuing Differences at Digital Equipment Corporation, find a simple illustration is worth a thousand words. Using three separate circles, Zimmerlee points out that EEO and valuing diversity are like "two circles that touch but don't overlap—the first representing the legal need for diversity, the second the corporate desire for diversity. Affirmative action is a third circle that overlaps the other two and holds them together with policies and procedures."[2]

Endorsing Diversity at the Top

Once the distinctions between EEO/AA and valuing diversity are made clear, senior managers and other visible leaders in the organization must begin to enthusiastically endorse the new philosophy. As such, they must make a concerted effort to talk about the benefits of increased diversity in formal and informal communications with their constituencies. Leaders must also be prepared to answer challenges from those employees who will question the timing or appropriateness of this change in human resources management strategy. In particular, they must be able respond to any allegations that suggest valuing diversity will lead to overpermissiveness or a lowering of organizational standards.

Generally, leaders committed to valuing diversity find ample opportunity to spread their message and express their support. Some, like Charles J. Many, president of NYNEX Mobile Communications Company (NMCC), begin with a formal statement to set the stage for change and make the connection between diversity and future organizational success. To underscore the importance of diversity at NMCC, Many asserted at a recent corporate management conference that "every company has access to essentially the same technology. Therefore, the key to success has to be the way NYNEX Mobile encourages, develops, and utilizes its employees' ideas and energies. *Every* employee's ideas and energies."

Some leaders also make the most of opportunities to publicly endorse diversity. For example, Chairman David T. Kearns of

Xerox Corporation is a visible advocate for diversity who is quoted regularly in the business press. While his exact words vary slightly in every article, Kearns' fundamental message continues to be, "the company that gets out in front managing diversity . . . will have a competitive edge."[3]

Articulating a Pluralistic Vision

As they set the stage for culture change, organizational leaders must help employees recognize the long-term need for valuing diversity and the potential benefits that it offers. In order to do this, they must articulate a vision of the organization's future that acknowledges the importance of valuing diversity. This pluralistic vision statement should emphasize the connection between achieving the organization's core mission and valuing diversity.

In some institutions, the creation of this goal or vision statement is regarded as the primary responsibility of those at the top. In others, this statement is created by a diverse employee task force and is then ratified by senior management, union officials, and so on. Regardless of which process is used, it is critical for organizational leaders to play an active role in shaping this vision statement. In order to fully support a pluralistic vision and help make it a reality, leaders must actively participate in its creation.

Once this pluralistic vision statement has been created and endorsed, it then serves as a commitment and long-range goal for the institution. Because it represents the future state in the culture change process, the vision statement helps employees appreciate where the organization is heading. It also describes what the organization will be like when the culture of diversity becomes a reality.

The following are two examples of vision statements that have been developed and endorsed by institutions committed to valuing diversity. The first is a corporate statement developed by employees at NYNEX Mobile Communications Company to reflect the organization's long-range focus on diversity in achieving business goals. It reads:

Because we must reflect the diverse society we serve, it is critical to our business that we become more diverse. Thus, as an organization, we are committed to creating a culture that promotes mutual respect, acceptance, cooperation, and productivity among people who are diverse in work background, education, age, gender, race, ethnic origin, physical abilities, religious beliefs, sexual/affectional orientation, and other perceived differences. Understanding and valuing differences will maximize the growth and development of our employees and meet the needs of our increasingly diverse customer base.

At Stanford University, where students, staff, and faculty are engaged in a long-term change process to encourage interactive pluralism, a written goal statement entitled "Building a Multiracial, Multicultural University Community" has been developed to direct and guide the change effort. Here are some brief excepts:

Having achieved a strong measure of racial diversity . . . we must now make a new commitment. We must make the transition from numerical diversity to interactive pluralism. We must define a new vision for the University as a community where all ethnic groups can engage their differences in a process of mutual enrichment. . . . We believe that gender, racial, ethnic, cultural, religious and other individual or group differences enrich the educational and social environment where we teach, learn, live and work. These differences, rather than inhibiting communication and concord, present us with singular opportunities to find mutual understanding and respect.[4]

Both of these statements contain three important characteristics found in the vision statements of many leading-edge organizations. First, they identify the specific goals that the organizations are striving to achieve. Second, diversity is discussed in broad, multidimensional terms that are both explicit and inclusive. Finally, the organizational benefits of valuing diversity are also clearly identified.

PHASE 2: EDUCATION AND CHANGE IMPLEMENTATION

Once the stage has been set by senior managers and other organizational leaders, a systematic process of awareness development and culture change can begin. While this implementation process includes many separate steps, several can occur concurrently. However, care should be taken *not* to initiate any other implementation steps until a critical mass of employees and managers has received awareness training and is prepared to support the culture change.

The following list describes major steps in Phase 2 of this blueprint for culture change:

- Providing awareness education to minimize culture clash and improve work relationships among all employees.

- Enlisting support for change from employees at all organizational levels.

- Diversifying work groups and decision-making groups.

- Creating benefit plans that reflect diverse employee priorities.

- Tying individual and group rewards to consistent behavior that values diversity.

- Creating structures to support organizational change.

- Developing coaching and tutoring mechanisms to enhance individual and work group effectiveness.

Providing Awareness Education

Given the profusion of training programs, audiovisual materials, and consulting services currently available, it is not surprising that many institutions have a difficult time deciding what to include in their valuing diversity educational efforts. Rather than recommend a specific curriculum, it will be more useful to consider three critical factors that influence the quality and effectiveness of valuing diversity training efforts in *all* organizations.

The first factor is the degree of involvement of organizational leaders in awareness training. Where this involvement is limited, with officers, union officials, and other leaders making an "appearance" at workshops but not participating, the impact of awareness training on culture change is *also* limited. Where leader involvement is equal to that of other employees, the potential impact is greater—assuming that the basic training is comprehensive. However, in most institutions, impact is greatest when those in key leadership positions receive considerably *more* awareness training than the average employee at the start of the culture change effort. This early, in-depth leadership education should focus on:

- Exploration of the primary dimensions of diversity.
- Analysis of the impact of assimilation on the ability of **others** to succeed.
- Exploration of personal values, stereotypes, and prejudices.
- Examination of the impact of destructive "isms" on **others.**
- Assessment of the organization's readiness to value diversity.
- Identification of current barriers that will impede the culture change process.

A second factor that should be considered in planning the training curriculum is the balance to be struck between intellectual and experimental learning. While a single focus on theories, principles, demographic changes, and the organizational benefits of increased diversity can produce lively intellectual discussion in seminars, it is less likely to cause individuals to examine their personal values, attitudes, and behaviors or actively support culture change. Conversely, training that focuses solely on emotional reactions to key issues such as **otherness,** personal stereotyping, collusion, and the nature of prejudice will sometimes produce considerable personal insight but is less likely to lead to institutional change. To support the culture of diversity, training and education must generate both heat *and* light. As such, seminars and workshops should address individual, group, and organizational issues that help and hinder the change process and engage participants at both the emotional and intellectual levels.

The third factor to consider in planning and developing awareness training is how extensive the curriculum should be. Based on the complexity of the subject, it is unlikely that many organizations will run out of appropriate training topics before exhausting available funding. Therefore, the difficult decision in curriculum planning is likely to be prioritizing the organization's most critical educational needs and deciding who to invite to what event(s). Where limited funding is a major factor, the rule of thumb is quite simple:

(1) Begin with leadership education.

(2) Follow up with general manager *and* employee education about stereotyping and the dimensions of diversity.

(3) Continue with ongoing seminars in managing diversity as a vital resource, developing pluralistic leadership skills, understanding the dimensions of diversity, career development/efficacy training for diverse employees, and so on.

In some organizations such as Hewlett-Packard Company, "managing diversity" training is modularized, electronically transmitted, and offered on an open enrollment basis. In other companies such as NYNEX Mobile Communications Company, basic "awareness training" is required for managers and available to employees at all levels. While every organization develops its own rationale for including and/or excluding various employee groups, the decision that appears to produce the best results is including *everyone* regardless of level in basic awareness training and then following up with specialized education for specific employee groups.

Enlisting Employee Support

Once awareness training begins, it is usually not long before some employees begin to ask, "What can I do to get more involved in this change process?" In some organizations, this question then leads to the formation of formal networks among employees of similar core identities. Where these networks have the support of the organization and are given a role as programmatic resources, they offer employees a means of ongoing involvement in efforts to shape the culture of diversity.

Occasionally, organizations also encourage employees to volunteer as awareness workshop facilitators—in order to spread the valuing diversity message and build grass roots support for change. When this occurs, volunteer facilitators who receive training as workshop leaders often become powerful agents of change—convincing the uncommitted in the organization of the value of diversity through their personal involvement and commitment.

For example, in 1990, within NYNEX Mobile Communications Company, an organization of approximately 1,200 employees, 26 volunteer facilitators paired up to deliver "Diversity at Work"—a one-day awareness workshop open to all employees. These volunteers included diverse employees from every level of the organization—few of whom had prior training experience. After attending a facilitator training session, each volunteer was paired with an **other** and scheduled to deliver two workshops. While the company expected that it would then need to ask for additional volunteers to meet the continued demand for training, this turned out not to be the case. Instead, most facilitators elected to remain involved, stating that volunteering as a trainer was the "best way to make a real difference."

Based on participant feedback, NMCC's volunteer core seems to be having a positive impact within the organization. As one employee stated, "Because they're employees first and facilitators second, I believe them when they say this is good for the company. I can also see they're personally sold on the value of diversity and that makes me a believer, too!"

Diversifying Work Groups and Decision-Making Groups

In addition to using education and volunteerism to foster change, institutions must also demonstrate their belief in the value of diversity by integrating work groups and decision-making groups at all levels and in all departments. It is in this area particularly that virtually *every organization in America* can continue to show improvement. Although the lack of a "qualified pool" of candidates may have posed a real barrier to increased diversity in the past, today it has become a very weak argument.

In organizations that claim to value diversity, the true depth of this commitment can be measured by examining the percentages of **others** in nontraditional, technical, and executive jobs. In cases where these numbers are increasing annually, the commitment to employee diversity is likely to be real. However, in cases where no increase occurs, there is reason to question the stated commitment to change.

While this assessment may seem arbitrary to some readers, it is the authors' firm belief that every institution in America can increase diversity in nontraditional, technical, and executive jobs now—*without* compromising performance standards or displacing mainstream employees. By demonstrating a commitment to diversity through their actions as well as in their words, employers are more likely to become true believers—as they reap the benefits of increased innovation and improved productivity.

For today, in many organizations, workforce diversity is beginning to have a positive effect on productivity. Diversification of work groups and decision-making groups is beginning to pay off in greater innovation and effective teamwork. For example, diversity seems to be helping teamwork and productivity in the automotive industry.

In 1988, the United Auto Workers Union (UAW) joined the management of General Motors and the Toyota Company to establish a new manufacturing organization—New United Motor Manufacturing, Inc. (NUMMI). Working together, these three diverse partners created a manufacturing operation that places greater emphasis on teamwork and increased flexibility.

The NUMMI plant also employs a diverse workforce including 28 percent Hispanic, 24 percent black, and 22 percent women employees.

Since opening for business, NUMMI has generated the highest productivity and quality levels in the GM system—levels comparable to those in Toyota's Japanese plants. According to Bruce Lee, a regional director of the UAW, the quality of the teamwork at NUMMI has benefited from employee diversity. As he stated in an interview for this book, "Having people from diverse cultures with differing ideas is a plus in the team concept process."

Enhancing Benefit Plans

While the value of work team diversity is becoming more apparent in leading-edge organizations, the need for flexible employee benefits is also on the rise. Unfortunately, most organizations continue to move slowly and with extreme caution in their efforts to satisfy this need. For example, after more than a decade of discussion about the shortage of quality day care in America, less than 5 percent of U.S. organizations now provide on-site care facilities. In addition, despite rising health-care costs, most institutions have actually been paring back their benefit programs as they increase the number of individual "options" available to employees. Even in some organizations with formal valuing diversity programs, employee benefits continue to be treated as separate and apart from this change.

While the trend among many employers seems to be towards more variety and less total value in benefit programs, some institutions are beginning to recognize that employee benefit plans *are an extension* of other efforts to value diversity. In addition, as competition for new workers intensifies in the 1990s and benefits become an increasingly important factor in employment decisions, *more, not less,* will need to be done to enhance benefit plans in order to attract and retain new employees.

Among the more creative responses to the need for flexible yet comprehensive employee benefits is the recent decision by some employers to offer extended-hour child care as a service to employees who work overtime and evening shifts. For example, at America West Airlines, where employee shifts run round the clock, a 24-hour, seven-day-a-week child-care facility is available near the company's Phoenix hub. After receiving complaints from employees who found it extremely difficult to arrange for child care that was adaptable to their fluctuating hours and work schedules, this company decided to solve the problem by providing the service in-house.[5]

America West's creative solution to a serious workplace problem underscores the point that employers often can do more than they are currently doing to assist employees through flexible, comprehensive benefit programs. A recent Gallup poll conducted for the Employee Benefit Research Institute also supports this point. According to the results, nearly three out of four Americans think employers can do "a lot more" to help employees be both good workers and good parents.[6] In the future, organizations committed to creating a culture of diversity will have to treat benefits as an integral part of the culture change process. As such, they will need to enhance rather than reduce the array of benefits offered—keeping in mind the increasingly diverse needs and lifestyles of all their employees.

Rewarding Behavior that Values Diversity

As efforts to create the culture of diversity evolve and expand, institutional reward systems used to motivate and recognize effective performance must also change. Once managers and supervisors are trained and prepared to manage diversity as a vital resource, the organization must begin to hold them accountable for doing this. As employees become more aware of the destructive nature of prejudice and stereotyping, they must also be prepared to respect **others,** cooperate in diverse work settings, and support the new philosophy of valuing diversity. Even in cases where employees do not personally endorse this philosophy, their workplace behavior should still be expected to support this change. To expect less than this is a serious mistake—one that can ultimately derail culture change.

Today, in organizations like Security Pacific Corporation, a company that has been involved in valuing diversity efforts for several years, employees at all levels are expected to "walk the talk" by demonstrating respect for **others** through their day-today actions. Starting with senior executives, where performance evaluation is directly tied to active support for this change, paying attention to diversity issues is considered to be an important part of every manager's job at Security Pacific.

In the future, as employee diversity continues to increase in the American workplace, the importance of working effectively with **others** will also increase. As this happens, employees who value differences will be far more likely to function effectively within diverse work groups. They will also be more likely to manage diversity as a vital resource and succeed as pluralistic leaders.

Creating Structures to Support Organizational Change

As organizations move towards creating a new, more inclusive culture of diversity, many recognize that new structures are required to guide and support this change. Among the structures that can be used to support culture change in support of diversity are:

- Employee networks.
- Diversity councils.
- Offices of diversity.

Within many organizations, employee networks are the first new structures to emerge in support of valuing diversity. As discussed earlier, these networks are usually created by employees and linked to a particular core dimension of diversity. For example, at U S West, there are many separate employee networks including organizations for American Indian, Asian, black, differently abled, gay and lesbian, Hispanic, Vietnam veteran, and women employees. Known as "resource groups," these employee networks serve as support groups and educational resources for their members and also function as sounding boards and feedback groups for the organization. They are typical of networks that are developing in institutions across the United States.

Among the other structures beginning to emerge in organizations committed to valuing diversity are diversity councils and offices of diversity. Unlike employee networks, these structures are usually created by the organization itself to encourage dialogue about workplace issues and to manage the overall change process. Diversity councils are often composed of volunteer representatives from employee networks and committed **others** who mirror the diversity that exists across an organization. They are usually recognized by the formal organization and encouraged to meet regularly in order to plan and stage activities for employees throughout the organization.

While the precise role of the diversity council varies within organizations, most are involved in the following activities:

- Exchanging information and publishing newsletters about employee network activities.

- Researching and circulating articles, books, and other educational materials for use throughout the organization.

- Conducting informal employee opinion surveys about diversity issues in the workplace.

- Sponsoring lunchtime and after-hours educational events.

- Functioning as formal sensing and feedback groups for the institution.

For example, at University of California, Los Angeles (UCLA) the chancellor has created a council on diversity which reports to him on a regular basis. Chaired by an associate vice chancellor, the council's main task is to make certain that women and people of color are well represented in all aspects of campus and academic life. To accomplish this, the council works to identify nontraditional students, faculty and others who can make a significant contribution on campus and help the university achieve its goal of valuing cultural diversity.

Unlike employee networks and diversity councils that are staffed by volunteers, the office of diversity is typically an organizational unit set up within the formal institution and staffed by full-time change agents and administrative personnel. Typically, this unit serves as the fulcrum for both volunteer-supported and organization-initiated programs, activities, and changes in support of valuing diversity. Although few organizations have reached the stage where they recognize the need for an office of diversity, there is little doubt that these units will multiply in the future as interest in this change continues to grow.

To maximize their impact, offices of diversity should be positioned to serve the needs of the entire organization. They must be staffed by employees who are both committed to the institution's pluralistic vision and able to challenge the organization and its leaders to move ahead with change. As such, the office of diversity should not be positioned as a regional or departmental function. It should not be part of the human resources department. Instead, it will be most credible and viable reporting directly to the office of the president and responsible for:

- Setting culture change strategy.
- Interpreting and modifying existing organizational policies.
- Creating additional policies in support of diversity.
- Educating the leadership of the organization.
- Consulting to key personnel on pluralistic leadership issues.
- Planning and managing the overall culture change with input and support from employees and with the ongoing advice and consent of the policy committee.

Typically, the decision to create an office of diversity grows out of the realization that culture change to support diversity must be carefully managed and not simply allowed to occur. When this office is used to guide and manage the change process, it helps to ensure that the institution remains on track and continues to move toward its ultimate goal. However, when it functions as an extension of the human resources department or another regional unit within the institution, it is not positioned for maximum effectiveness.

Developing Coaching and Tutoring Mechanisms

In addition to institutional change, valuing diversity also requires that changes occur at the individual and work group levels. It is in these areas that coaching and tutoring programs can be particularly useful. As we begin this discussion, it is important to note the important distinction that exists between coaching and another, immensely popular but less useful mechanism commonly referred to as *mentoring*.

In recent years, much has been written about mentoring as a philosophy, a function, and an organizational art. While some researchers claim that a mentor or powerful personal adviser is critical for individual career success, other analysts insist that the importance of mentoring has been greatly exaggerated. In the view of the authors, neither claim is correct. For while mentors are still enormously important for select individuals in organizations that value homogeneity, they are anachronistic and often counterproductive in those that value employee diversity.

Historically, within homogeneous institutions, mentoring has been the dominant group's method of informal succession planning. As such, those in power routinely selected others of similar core identity, shared insider information with them about unstated rules and norms, provided one-on-one counseling and, generally, helped select individuals to move ahead. Like some traditional father-son relationships, mentoring helped to preserve the established order by concentrating organizational power in the hands of the dominant group. While this process of "natural selection" went on in virtually every institution in America, it was seldom discussed or challenged.

Then, during the 1970s, as culture clash increased and **others** began to challenge mainstream traditions, this mentoring process came under intense scrutiny. By the 1980s, mentoring came to be viewed as a critical ingredient in the formula for career success. Therefore, in many organizations it was deemed crucial that **others** be given mentors to assure their future success.

Since then, diverse employees, researchers, change agents, executives, and many institutions committed to valuing diversity have tried to reconstitute the original mentor relationship of old—with limited success. As one participant in a corporate mentoring program recently stated, "Even though we're both trying to make this relationship work, it feels awkward and forced—like an arranged marriage." It is not just a lack of personal chemistry that makes formal mentoring difficult in organizations committed to valuing diversity—it is also the inherent contradiction in old versus new values that mentoring underscores.

Historically, in organizations that did not value diversity, mentoring helped the dominant group preserve the status quo, share insider information, and perpetuate the homogeneous ideal. It was an exclusive rather than inclusive strategy that promoted elitism, secrecy, and manipulation. As such, the essential purpose behind mentoring worked *in opposition to* the philosophy of valuing diversity. For this reason, it is time for organizations to abandon mentoring as a strategy for valuing diversity and acknowledge it for what it is—a vestige of the past and *not* the key to a more productive future.

Unlike mentoring, informal coaching and tutoring programs do not hinge on the creation of exclusive, one-on-one relationships. They do not presume that there are unstated "rules" or norms in the organization that only a select group of insiders should know about or discuss. Instead, they are inclusive mechanisms for individual change that focus on technical, interpersonal, and managerial skill development.

By tapping the skills of employees at all levels—who volunteer as advisers, coaches, and tutors—these programs can utilize the talents and energies of many. They can also provide participants with the technical assistance, interpersonal feedback, and personal attention required for increased comfort and improved performance.

PHASE 3: ONGOING MAINTENANCE ACTIVITIES

Once valuing diversity has been institutionalized through the creation of formal structures, the vitality of the culture change effort must then be maintained. To accomplish this goal over time, the office of diversity must be responsible for developing and overseeing follow-up activities that ensure that valuing employee diversity remains a high priority. These activities should include:

- Periodic cultural audits that examine organizational practices, norms, and so on, and their impact on diverse employees.

- Periodic employee opinion surveys to identify emerging diversity issues and measure effectiveness of current activities.

- Annual survey feedback for individual managers identifying specific pluralistic leadership strengths and areas for improvement.

For these ongoing programs to be successful, managers and employees at all levels must actively participate. Likewise, it is the responsibility of every department in the organization to complement and supplement the activities of the office of diversity with local initiatives, including:

- Basic awareness training for new employees and advanced seminars for others with an interest in expanding their understanding of the primary and secondary dimensions of diversity.

- Continuous monitoring of recruitment, hiring, development, and promotion trends to assure that these reflect the organization's continued commitment to the value of employee diversity.

ACHIEVING THE ULTIMATE GOAL

To create the culture of diversity, organizations must be willing and able to move *beyond* where they are today. They need to critically examine their fundamental values as they examine their traditions and unspoken assumptions about managing **others.** They need to ask themselves what attitudes and behaviors the current culture rewards and discourages. Where they find disparities between their stated commitment to diversity and the day-to-day realities, they must work to close these gaps.

When valuing diversity becomes the norm, not the exception; when **others** are part of the mainstream and no longer on the periphery; when the organization *automatically* utilizes the talents of all employees—then the ultimate goal will finally be achieved, and full and lasting benefits of the culture of diversity will be apparent to everyone.

NOTES

1. Mikhail Gorbachev, *Perestroika* (New York: Harper & Row, 1988), p. 15.
2. R. Roosevelt Thomas, Jr., "From Affirmative Action to Affirming Diversity," *Harvard Business Review*, March–April 1990, p. 111.
3. Sharon Nelton, "Meet Your New Work Force," *Nation's Business*, July 1988, p. 15.
4. Stanford University Self-Study on Building a Multiracial Multicultural University Community, Stanford University, April 1990. pp. 1–4.
5. Cathy Trost, "Creative Child Care Programs Aid Employees Who Work Odd Hours," *The Wall Street Journal*, March 18, 1988, p. 21.
6. Selwyn Feinstein, "Labor Letter," *The Wall Street Journal*, February 13, 1990, p. 1.

Chapter Twelve

Workplace 2000: From Assimilation to Valuing Diversity

*"The hard and stiff will be broken
The soft and supple will prevail."*[1]

Lao Tzu, Philosopher and Writer

W e began this book with a visit to a policy committee meeting at Home Products, Inc. (HPI), a "typical" American company in the year 2000. For a brief moment, let us take you back to the future to the same meeting as it winds down. As you join the group, Carl Philips, VP of marketing, is discussing the marketing program for BRITE—the company's new detergent product.

"Without a doubt, it's the most sophisticated targeted marketing plan we've every developed," he states. "We've got special programs for every diverse consumer group. And we've already received some very positive feedback about the new campaign from several of the company's employee networks.

"Both the Hispanic Network and the Gay Alliance told us they like the tone and the message in our targeted programs. You know, *all* the employee networks gave us a lot of help in pulling this campaign together. Their suggestions and feedback really made the program sing. Thanks largely to their input, we've got a program that is guaranteed to drive consumers into the stores. Personally, I couldn't be more pleased!"

"Thanks, Carl," says President Mary McKenzie. "And by the way, I agree with you. It's our strongest marketing program yet—because it reaches all our key target groups. When the diversity council meets next week, I'd like to attend the session so I can give them my personal thanks for all their help!"

Changing topics, McKenzie continues, "Before we conclude this meeting, I'd like to cover the last item on our agenda—the expanded hours at our dependent-care facility. As of today, our on-site facility will be open round the clock—to accommodate all our employees, including those on the new night shift. To mark the occasion, I've been invited to city hall this afternoon for a press conference with the board of supervisors. Apparently, they're interested in focusing attention on our dependent-care facility—in order to interest other companies in opening similar centers."

A COMMITMENT TO DIVERSITY

You're impressed! As part of its continuing commitment to employee diversity, HPI is about to be publicly recognized for taking a leadership role in the area of enhanced employee benefits. What's more, in the past five years, it has received more than a dozen citations and awards for similar innovations.

Back in 1990, when the company was less than half its current size, HPI made a serious commitment to valuing employee diversity—believing that this change was not only good for the business, it was also good for employees. Since that time, HPI has worked hard to develop a culture of diversity with both the organizational leaders and employees getting deeply involved in this effort.

To set the stage for culture change back in 1990, the corporation ran a series of executive briefings for its officers, senior line managers, and top union officials. Then, the following year, training was expanded and offered to all employees. At the same time, employee networks began to develop within the company. Rather than ignore these groups, HPI offered each network modest financial support plus the use of the company's electronic communications systems and reproduction services. Later on, at the suggestion of senior management, a diversity council was established to coordinate employee network activities and provide formal feedback about diversity issues to all corporate officers.

Today, HPI's office of diversity is responsible for maintaining and updating all diversity training programs and supporting the continuing process of culture change through corporate policy development, the management of employee opinion survey feedback, and other efforts aimed at increasing honest communication, mutual respect, and cooperation among all employees.

CLINGING TO THE HOMOGENEOUS IDEAL

The policy committee meeting continues, but you must move on. You have another appointment at OR&C, a competitive organization just down the street. Quietly, you gather your things and slip out the back door. As you arrive at your next destination, you can't help but notice the difference in the makeup of the meeting. Unlike the group at HPI, OR&C's executive committee is composed almost exclusively of white men. Out of a group of 12 corporate officers, there is just one person of color and one woman.

As you look around the conference table at the solemn faces, you find yourself comparing the atmosphere of this meeting with the one you just left. "This is certainly a different kind of organization!" you think to yourself. Then you listen as the CFO begins his report.

"Unfortunately, gentlemen, the sales decline for the past quarter has turned out to be even steeper than we originally projected. The continuing quality control problems we've been having at our Dayton plant have caused us to slip into a serious back-order situation. And that's not all. We've also . . . ."

Before the CFO can go on, the president jumps in. "Al, I'm really concerned about what's going to happen when the analysts get hold of this information. As you well know, our stock is already taking a beating on the exchange. Our persistent labor problems and lack of new product success are becoming major issues in the business press. Frankly, I'm afraid this new problem in Dayton is going to put us in a very vulnerable position."

"That may be the understatement of the year!" exclaims the general counsel. "The Clarion Investment Group has already accumulated 25 percent of our outstanding shares. When this news hits the street, it may be just the ammunition they need to pull off their tender offer. This time next year, we could all be working for Clarion! That is, if we're still working at all!"

THE FAILURE OF ASSIMILATION

The CFO continues his presentation, but you've already heard enough. Clearly, OR&C is a company in serious trouble. During the decade of the 90s, it did little to value employee diversity. Instead, the corporate policy remained "treat employees as if they're the same." In the opinion of senior management, focusing on differences was counterproductive. Besides, the only problem the company ever had with diverse employees was controlling the "militant" ones who refused to cooperate. Today, instead of capitalizing on the innovation and energy that diversity could have offered, the officers of OR&C must now focus on short-term survival.

As we leave the future and return to the present, it goes without saying that precise predictions about the next decade, or even the next week, are impossible to make. Nonetheless, the broad parameters of the American workplace of the future are already taking shape. Based on these emerging parameters, it is becoming clear that by the year 2000, organizations that wish to prosper will have no alternative—they will have to have embraced the concept of diversity completely and enthusiastically.

LONG–TERM BENEFITS OF DIVERSITY

Embracing diversity will require a willingness to invest the time and effort required to understand concepts like the dimensions of diversity, the homogeneous ideal, the strategy of assimilation, stereotyping, cultural myopia, collusion, garbled communication, culture clash, and the need for common ground.

Although this effort will take energy and commitment, it will result in significant long-term advantages for those organizations willing to make the necessary investment.

Foremost among these long-term advantages will be:

- The full utilization of the organization's human capital.

- Reduced interpersonal conflict among **others** as respect for diversity increases.

- Enhanced work relationships based on mutual respect and increased employee knowledge of multicultural issues.

- A shared organizational vision and increased commitment among diverse employees at all organizational levels and across all functions.

- Greater innovation and flexibility as **others** participate more fully in key decision-making and problem-solving groups.

- Improved productivity as more employee effort is directed at accomplishing tasks and less energy is spent managing interpersonal conflicts and culture clash.

THE DOWNSIDE OF "BUSINESS AS USUAL"

At the same time, for those organizations that do not step up to the challenge of valuing a diverse workforce now, the problems in the future will be persistent and severe. In particular, these institutions are likely to be plagued by:

- High turnover among **others** as many employees opt out in search of a more supportive work environment.

- Low morale among those who remain due to persistent culture clash and on-going conflicts between many mainstream employees and **others.**

- Limited innovation due to over-reliance on "tried and true" methods and the underutilization of the skills and perspectives of **others.**

- Lagging productivity as mainstream employees and **others** remain locked in intergroup conflicts that impede their ability to work together and impair their effectiveness in dealing with diverse customers.

- Growing inability to recruit the best and the brightest new workers as the organization's divisive image and reputation precede it into the employment market place.

THE EMERGING NEW ORDER

When Alvin Toffler's *Future Shock* was published 20 years ago, the author spoke of a "finely fragmented social order—a super-industrial order—based on diversity of products and people." He noted that "the powerful bonds that integrated industrial society—bonds of law, common values, centralized and standardized education, and cultural production—were breaking down."[2] He also noted that we had not yet learned how to link the fragmented pieces of the new social order together—how to integrate them into a meaningful whole.

The purpose of this book is to provide insights into that linking process—in the office, the executive suite, at the union bargaining table, in government agencies, and in educational institutions. For although valuing diversity is still very new, and trial and error remain the order of the day, proven techniques and approaches are beginning to emerge.

In the future, these ground-breaking efforts must continue. In fact, within organizations that are focused on the future, efforts to create the culture of diversity need to *increase*. The need for organizational culture change must be acknowledged and no longer denied. For those institutions that deny this new reality will be setting themselves up for a costly and tragic failure.

DANGERS OF DENIAL

Today, the "head-in-the-sand" mentality exhibited by many institutions calls to mind the image of the ancient dinosaurs. These mighty creatures eventually faced extinction because of their inability to change. Individuals and organizations who wait for concrete proof that they need to embrace diversity risk suffering a similar fate. By adopting a policy of "wait and see," they risk being overwhelmed by their competitors as they fail at the task of attracting and retaining diverse employees.

But while the dinosaurs' inability to adapt was built into their genetic programming, organizations have no such limitations. Their only restrictions are the vision and commitment of their leaders and their own ability to tap the diverse talents of every employee. One cannot ignore the increasing probability that leaders who fail to value diversity now, will cease being leaders in the future. What's more, organizations that refuse to accept this change will also be at enormous risk.

COMPLEX PROBLEMS/MULTIPLE SOLUTIONS

As humankind confronts the complex economic and social problems of the next millennium and as new issues emerge and confound the old systems, a single, homogenized approach to management and problem solving will be far less likely to succeed. Instead, creative solutions will be far more likely to come from a broad, deep pool of diverse talents, perspectives, and life experiences. As such, it is the richness of employee diversity that will ultimately lead to innovation and productive change in the future.

Today, the American workplace is at a crossroads. The two visions described earlier in this chapter are two possible futures that await us. As this book has attempted to point out, we must choose wisely if we are to prosper. We must depart from the old, worn, familiar road and set out enthusiastically down a new path towards the culture of diversity. For although this path may be unfamiliar and bumpy, at its end lies a more creative, productive, and humane workplace—not only for **others,** but for us all.

NOTES

1. Lao Tzu, *Tao Te Ching* (New York: Harper & Row, 1988), p. 76.
2. Alvin Toffler, *Future Shock* (New York: Bantam Books, 1970), p. 301.

Chapter Synopses

CHAPTER ONE: DIVERSITY IN THE 90s

Massive demographic changes occurring in the American workplace are creating new challenges for managers. To succeed in the future, they will have to replace the "cookie cutter" approach to managing human resources in which employee diversity is ignored or devalued with one that views diversity as a vital resource. New attitudes and skills will be required to hire and develop diverse employees and to lead diverse organizations. In particular, there needs to be a shift in focus away from a homogeneous view of employees towards a pluralistic view. To make this shift, managers will need to:

1. Recognize cultural diversity.

2. Learn to value and respect fundamental differences.

3. Find common ground on which to build relationships of trust and mutual respect with diverse employees.

CHAPTER TWO: DIMENSIONS OF DIVERSITY

From a subjective, personal point-of-view, diversity is **otherness** or those human qualities that are different from our own and outside the groups to which we belong. Objectively speaking, diversity is a complex set of primary and secondary human dimensions or variables that shape our values, experiences, and behavior. Primary dimensions are those immutable differences that exert an important impact on us throughout life. The primary dimensions help form our core identities and, minimally, include: age, ethnicity, gender, physical abilities/qualities, race, and sexual/affectional orientation.

Secondary dimensions of diversity are often more mutable. Some exert an impact on us as we grow and develop, others affect us more as adults. These dimensions of human difference include but are not limited to: educational background, geographic location, income, marital status, military experience, parental status, religious beliefs, and work experience. Some secondary dimensions can be modified throughout life. Others may have such a powerful impact on individuals and groups that they become primary.

While differences in core identities result in diverse expectations, priorities and concerns, most U.S. organizations refused to recognize employee diversity in the past. Instead of acknowledging the impact of the dimensions of diversity on the attitudes and behavior of employees, institutions assumed that diversity should be ignored and that equal treatment in the workplace meant the same treatment for every employee.

This oversimplification has led to attempts by institutions to change diverse employees or **others** (those who do not fit the profile of the dominant group) so that they can assimilate into the mainstream culture. Yet, it is **otherness** itself that represents America's greatest untapped creative resource.

In today's increasingly complex and competitive environment, **otherness** or diversity represents an enormous source of new ideas and vitality. Those organizations that learn to value employee diversity and manage it as an asset will be far more likely to flourish in the future. Those that continue to view **otherness** as a liability will be far more likely to fail.

CHAPTER THREE: THE DYNAMICS OF ASSIMILATION

Throughout the American workplace, assimilation has been the traditional strategy used to manage employee diversity. A homogeneous culture (which values sameness and not diversity) has been the result.

Five characteristics are commonly found in organizations that value homogeneity and use the strategy of assimilation to manage diversity. These include:

1. The dominant group's standards are universally applied.

2. The competence of diverse employees is continuously tested.

3. Informal communication networks are closed to **others.**

4. Key decision-making bodies are closed to **others.**

5. Support groups for **others** are discouraged.

The impact of assimilation on **others** results in: pressure to conform; role confusion; exclusion and isolation; and on-going tension. Likewise, assimilation impacts the dominant group by perpetuating the myth of the rugged individual and reinforcing the assumption that **others** are not qualified to succeed. Because assimilation reinforces the *rightness* of the dominant group's values, it often causes cultural myopia or the misguided belief that the dominant group's culture is relevant to all **others.** However, once cultural myopia is recognized, individuals can begin to take steps to overcome this perceptual problem.

CHAPTER FOUR: BEYOND STEREOTYPES: DEVELOPING AUTHENTIC RELATIONSHIPS WITH DIVERSE OTHERS

Stereotypes are rigid, distorted generalizations about all members of a particular group. Stereotypes are frequently used to reinforce an underlying prejudice about **others.** Prejudices are judgments made about **others** that reinforce a superiority/inferiority belief system. Prejudices foster the destructive "isms" (including ageism, ethnocentrism, heterosexism, racism, sexism, and so on) when they are combined with institutional power and used to systematically disadvantage **others.**

Regardless of how hard we may try to remain objective, everyone develops some prejudices and stereotypes about **others** as a result of early socialization. However, prejudices can be managed and their negative impact minimized by following a five step process:

1. Accepting responsibility for the problem.
2. Identifying problem behaviors.
3. Assessing the impact of problem behaviors on **others**.
4. Modifying negative behavior.
5. Obtaining feedback from **others**.

Once we acknowledge and learn to manage our prejudices, it becomes easier to recognize and appreciate differences without stereotyping **others**. Whereas stereotypes and prejudices discount and delimit **others,** acknowledgment supports the legitimacy and value of diversity.

CHAPTER FIVE: DECODING GARBLED COMMUNICATION

Language can play a powerful part in reinforcing stereotypes and garbling communication. To avoid this, managers need to heighten their language sensitivity and avoid using terms and expressions that ignore or devalue **others**. Managers also need to become familiar with the eleven elements of personal communication style and the many ways in which communication styles vary among individuals and diverse groups.

Managers can improve the quality and clarity of their communications with others by following these four steps:

1. Identify the specific elements of one's own communication style.
2. Recognize personal filters and test assumptions in cross-cultural communications.

3. Acknowledge one's own style when communicating with **others**.

4. Be aware of differences in cultural context.

Garbled communication is less likely to occur if managers assume they are communicating with **others** in all interactions and, therefore, remain sensitive to their own language usage as well as to stylistic differences.

CHAPTER SIX: UNDERSTANDING GROUP DYNAMICS AND MINIMIZING COLLUSION

Diversity in the workplace not only affects one-on-one relationships. Diversity also affects group dynamics or the patterns of interaction within work groups that help or hinder the accomplishment of tasks. Four factors have a particularly strong impact on the effective functioning of diverse work groups including: open membership, shared influence, mutual respect, and candor.

Collusion is an insidious dynamic that can decrease productivity and damage morale in diverse work groups. Collusion is conscious and unconscious cooperation among group members that reinforces stereotypic attitudes, behaviors and prevailing norms. People collude through silence, denial, and active cooperation. Fear of rejection or reprisal is often the motivation.

In order to break collusive behavior patterns, individuals need to:

- Seek assistance from **others** in identifying patterns of collusive behaviors.

- Begin by modifying collusive behavior in low-risk situations.

- Introduce the concept of collusion into the work group to raise awareness regarding this dynamic.

CHAPTER SEVEN: MANAGING CULTURE CLASH

Culture clash is conflict over basic values that occurs between groups of different core identities. This usually occurs in the workplace when the values, attitudes and behaviors of the dominant group are questioned by **others**. As organizations move away from assimilation towards the philosophy of valuing diversity, they are likely to experience some culture clash.

There are three types of culture clash:

1. Threatening.

2. Confusing.

3. Enhancing.

Common reactions among dominant group members to threatening culture clash include avoidance, denial and defensiveness. In confusing culture clashes, dominant group members may seek more information in an attempt to redefine the problem. When culture clash is perceived to be enhancing, members of the dominant group react with heightened anticipation, awareness, and proaction.

Culture clash is not static. Over time, a culture clash can evolve from threatening to confusing to enhancing. As it evolves, the strategies used to manage it must also evolve. Threatening and confusing culture clash can be minimized when diversity is understood and valued in an organization.

CHAPTER EIGHT: ESTABLISHING COMMON GROUND

Common ground is a shared set of assumptions that provides the basis for all cooperative action within diverse organizations. Establishing common ground requires that organizations move away from assimilation as a strategy for managing employee diversity towards greater differentiation and, finally, to integration. True integration cannot occur until the organization culture becomes one that values and supports diversity.

To create the culture of diversity, **others** must play an active role in shaping organizational standards and expectations. However, the major responsibility for this change rests with those in the dominant group who possess greater organizational power.

Efforts to establish common ground can be derailed due to inappropriate sequencing; insufficient resource allocation and lack of executive education. There is no "quick fix" approach to culture change or to establishing common ground. This process requires sustained effort over several years.

CHAPTER NINE: VALUING DIVERSITY IN LEADING-EDGE ORGANIZATIONS

Leading-edge organizations are those with a declared commitment to the philosophy of valuing diversity. Today, these organizations are engaged in a variety of educational and culture change efforts to institutionalize this philosophy and, thereby, to manage employee diversity as a vital resource.

Generally, leading-edge organizations share three characteristics including:

1. Commitment to the value of diversity among senior management.

2. A "different but equal" operating philosophy.

3. Expanded definitions of effective performance.

Leading-edge organizations also share several basic assumptions including:

- Employee diversity is a competitive advantage.

- The organization is in transition.

- Change the culture not the people.

There are several practices common to leading-edge organizations. These include:

- Linking diversity to the strategic vision.

- Management responsibility for climate setting.

- Systems and procedures that support diversity.
- Monitoring of recruitment, development, and promotion trends.
- Technical reeducation.
- Awareness education.
- Rewards based on performance results.
- Enhanced benefits.
- Reinforcement of the value of diversity in hiring and promotions.
- Attention to subtle reinforcers of the homogeneous ideal.

Together, these practices help to increase the presence of **others** in visible leadership roles; increase the voice of **others** as resources in efforts to change the organization's culture; increase employee interest and involvement in integrated networks.

CHAPTER TEN: THE PLURALISTIC LEADER

Pluralistic leaders are those who empower diverse employees and who are actively involved in efforts to create the culture of diversity within their organizations. In particular, pluralistic leaders exhibit six important qualities. These include:

1. An organizational vision and values that recognize and support employee diversity.

2. An ethical commitment to fairness and to the elimination of all types of workplace discrimination.

3. Broad knowledge and awareness regarding the primary and secondary dimensions of diversity and multicultural issues.

4. Openness to change based on diverse input and feedback about personal filters and blindspots.

5. Mentor and empowerer of diverse employees.

6. Sustained involvement as a catalyst and model for individual and organizational change in support of the value of diversity.

CHAPTER ELEVEN: CREATING ORGANIZATIONAL CULTURES THAT VALUE DIVERSITY

The culture of diversity is an institutional environment built on the values of fairness, diversity, mutual respect, understanding, and cooperation; where shared goals, rewards, performance standards, operating norms, and a common vision of the future guide the efforts of every employee and manager. The blueprint for creating this culture consists of a three-phase process. Key actions in each phase are described below.

Phase 1: Setting the Stage

- Acknowledging the fundamental difference between equal employment opportunity and valuing diversity.

- Endorsing the value of diversity at the top and communicating this throughout the organization.

- Articulating a pluralistic vision.

Phase 2: Education and Change Implementation

- Providing awareness education to minimize culture clash and improve work relationships.

- Enlisting support for change from employees at all organizational levels.

- Diversifying work groups and decision-making groups.

- Creating benefit plans that reflect diverse employee priorities.

- Tying individual and group rewards to consistent behavior that values diversity.

- Creating structures to support organizational change.

- Developing coaching and tutoring mechanisms to enhance individual and work group effectiveness.

Phase 3: On-Going Maintenance Activities

- Periodic cultural audits.

- Periodic employee opinion surveys.

- Annual survey feedback for managers.

- Awareness training.

- Continuous monitoring of recruitment, hiring, development, and promotion trends.

CHAPTER TWELVE: WORKPLACE 2000: FROM ASSIMILATION TO DIVERSITY AT WORK

Organizations committed to valuing diversity now can look forward to reaping substantial long-term rewards in the future. Foremost among these benefits will be:

- Full utilization of human capital.

- Reduced interpersonal conflict.

- Enhanced work relationships.

- Shared organizational vision and increased commitment among diverse employees.

- Greater innovation and flexibility.

On the other hand, those organizations that continue to view diversity as a liability are more likely to be plagued by:

- High turnover among **others.**

- Low employee morale.

- Limited innovation.

- Lagging productivity.

- Increased inability to recruit the most talented new workers.

Bibliography

C urrently, the literature on valuing and managing diversity is limited. Since the topic is relatively new and is not associated with any one discipline, references are scattered among a wide variety of books, academic journals, newspapers, and magazine articles. In some of the books listed, there are extensive bibliographies that can be used as additional resources.

AGE

Barron, Milton L. "The Aged as a Quasi-Minority Group." In *The Aging American: An Introduction to Social Gerontology and Geriatrics.* New York: Thomas Y. Crowell, 1961.
    Describes evidence of worldwide employer discrimination against the aged, reasons for it, and legislation against such practices. Although this book is dated, it contains useful information.

"Double Damages for Indifference to ADEA." *Fair Employment Practices.* Washington, D.C.: The Bureau of National Affairs, Inc., May 25, 1989.
    Discusses a legal application of the Age Discrimination in Employment Act in which an older worker fired for economic reasons was awarded double damages.

Hirsch, James S. "Older Workers Chafe under Young Managers." *The Wall Street Journal,* February 26, 1990, p. B1.
    Discusses how the 3.4 million over-65 workers in the United States create unique problems and opportunities for themselves and their corporations.

Knowles, Daniel E. "Dispelling Myths about Older Workers." In *Employing Older Americans: Opportunities and Constraints.* Report No. 916, ed., H. Axel. New York: Conference Board, 1988.
    Discusses ways to convince corporate America that older employees are and can remain competitive.

233

Mead, Margaret. *Culture and Commitment, A Study of the Generation Gap.* Garden City, N.Y.: Doubleday, 1970.

Discussion of reasons for differences in views and perspectives between younger and older people.

Scott-Marxell, Florida P. *The Measure of My Days.* New York: Aflred A. Knopf, 1968.

A personal perspective about life as an elderly woman by an 85-year-old writer, suffragette, and clinical psychologist.

COMMUNICATION

Applegate, Jane. "Mixed Signals: Mainstream Firms Must Learn to Adapt When Doing Business with American Indians." *Los Angeles Times,* August 17, 1989, Part IV, p. 1.

Describes communication barriers between American Indians and others.

Asante, Molefi K., and Alice Davis. "Encounters in the Interracial Workplace." in *Handbook of International and Intercultural Communication,* ed. M. Asante and W. Gudykunst. Beverly Hills, Calif.: Sage Publications, 1989, pp. 374–91.

A technical discussion of interracial communication in the context of situations, cultures, and experiences.

Birdsall, Paige. "A Comparative Analysis of Male and Female Managerial Communication Styles in Two Organizations." *Journal of Vocational Behavior* 16 (1980), pp. 183–96.

Describes results of a study of gender communication differences when managers communicate with subordinates.

Gudykunst, William B., and Young Y. Kim. *Communicating with Strangers: An Approach to Intercultural Communication.* New York: Random House, 1984.

A theoretical analysis of intercultural communication for those who communicate with people from other cultures as part of their job. Extensive bibliography.

Henley, Nancy. "Tactual Politics: Touch." in *Body Politics.* Englewood Cliffs, N.J.: Prentice Hall, 1977, pp. 94–110.

Examples, questionnaires, and studies of the use of touch between the sexes to gain or maintain power in a social hierarchy.

Jamison, Kaleel. "Sexism as Rank Language." *Social Change* Vol. 5, no. 2, p. 71.

A psychologically oriented discussion of the use of sexist language to indicate power.

Monroe, Linda R. "Cultural Shock Hits Health Care." *Los Angeles Times,* August 19, 1989, Part I, p. 1.

A discussion of how cultural information gaps interfere with constructive communication between health-care workers and patients.

Njeri, Itabari. "Intercultural Etiquette: When Different Groups Converge, the Ignorant and the Curious Can Be Unexpectedly Rude." *Los Angeles Times,* April 2, 1989, Part VI, p. 1.

A discussion of ways racist or culturally insensitive remarks, common in our increasingly diverse society, should be countered with education and common sense.

Pearson, Judy C. *Gender and Communication.* Dubuque, Iowa: Wm. C. Brown, 1985, pp. 6–32.

A discussion of the difficulties and differences in communication between men and women.

Rich, Andrea L. *Interracial Communication.* New York: Harper & Row, 1974.

A discussion of various forms of and reasons for interracial and interethnic communication gaps.

Schachter, Jim. "English Is Common Thread at S.F. Firm." *Los Angeles Times,* April 17, 1989.

Describes how classes in English conducted within a women's clothing company facilitate intercultural communications.

Solomon, Jolie. "Firms Grapple with Language Barriers: Diverse Workers Find Assistance and Resistance." *The Wall Street Journal,* November 7, 1989, p. B1.

A discussion of the culturally diverse workplace, describing corporate activities on bilingualism and other language issues.

Vetterling-Braggin, Mary, ed. *Sexist Language: A Modern Philosophical Analysis.* Totowa, N.J.: Littlefield, Adams, 1981.

A discussion of sexism and racism in language.

CULTURAL DIVERSITY

Adler, Nancy J. "Cultural Synergy: Managing the Impact of Cultural Diversity." In *The 1986 Annual: Developing Human Resources.* San Diego, Calif.: University Associates, 1986, pp. 229–38.

Reviews international studies of multiculturalism and proposes a model that can be used to explain diversity for organizational gain.

_____. *International Dimensions of Organizational Behavior.* Boston: Kent Publishing, 1986.

Discusses the ways cultural diversity impacts internal organizational operations and proposes strategies for viewing cultural diversity as a resource.

Copeland, Lennie. "Valuing Diversity, Part 1: Making the Most of Cultural Differences at the Workplace." *Personnel,* June 1988, pp. 52–60; "Valuing Diversity, Part 2: Pioneers and Champions of Change." *Personnel,* July 1988, pp. 44–49.

A look at the organizational impact of cultural diversity, with examples.

Ehrlich, Elizabeth, and Susan B. Garland. "For American Business, a New World of Workers." *Business Week*, September 19, 1988, pp. 112–20.

A special report on what companies are doing and will have to do to attract employees from a diverse workpool.

Gardenswartz, Lee, and Anita Rowe. "The Multi-Cultural Workforce." *Working World*. May 16, 1989, p. 16; June 26, 1989, p. 34; August 14, 1989, p. 20.

The three-part series that includes an organizational multicultural report card and 10 strategies for change.

Gudykunst, William B., and Young Y. Kim. *Communicating with Strangers: An Approach to Intercultural Communication*. New York: Random House, 1984.

A theoretical analysis of intercultural communication for those who communicate with people from other cultures as part of their job. Extensive bibliography.

Gurwitt, Rob. "How we spent the 1980s: A Pre-Census Look at a Changing America." *Governing*, August 1989, pp. 26–33.

A demographic look at the effects of immigration, population aging, and changing metropolitan ethnicity on U.S. cities.

Harris, Philip, R., and Robert T. Moran. *Managing Cultural Differences*. 2nd ed. Houston: Gulf Publishing, 1987.

A discussion of organizational cultural diversity that focuses on domestic and international perspectives, assimilation, and capitalizing on diversity.

Hispanic Business. October 1989.

This issue of *Hispanic Business* has several articles on corporate activities in cultural diversity, with emphasis on Hispanics.

Hymowitz, Carol. "One Firm's Bid to Keep Blacks, Women: Corning Battles to Overcome Ingrained Biases." *The Wall Street Journal*, February 16, 1989, p. B1.

Example of a typical U.S. firm's shift to valuing diversity; includes survey data on gender imbalance.

Johnston, William B., and Arnold E. Packer. *Workforce 2000: Work and Workers for the Twenty-first Century*. Indianapolis: Hudson Institute, June 1987.

Report produced for the U.S. Department of Labor that predicts what the U.S. labor market will look like in the year 2000. Tables and charts.

Nelton, Sharon. "Meet Your New Work Force." *Nation's Business*. July 1988, pp. 2–7.

A discussion of *Workforce 2000* that includes examples of corporate strategies, sources of help, and a discussion of language policies.

Schachter, Jim. "Firms Begin to Embrace Diversity." *Los Angeles Times*, April 17, 1988, Part 1, p. 1.

A discussion of *Workforce 2000* that includes corporate examples, programs for effecting change, and a discussion of the usefulness of diversity programs.

DIFFERENTLY ABLED

"Awards for Hiring the Disabled." *Fair Employment Practices.* Washington, D.C.: The Bureau of National Affairs, Inc., May 25, 1989, p. 63.

A description of corporate activities that won awards from the President's Committee on Employment of People with Disabilities.

Barker, Roger G. *Adjustment to Physical Handicap and Illness: A Survey of the Social Psychology of Physique and Disability.* New York: Social Science Research Council, 1953.

A theoretical and practical discussion of the social psychology of differently abled people, with a chapter on employment.

Biller, Ernest F. *Career Decision Making for Adolescents and Young Adults with Learning Disabilities.* Springfield, Ill.: Charles C. Thomas, 1987.

A discussion of theory, research, and practice in the process of career decision making for differently abled adolescents and young adults.

Biller, Ernest F. *Understanding Adolescents and Young Adults with Learning Disabilities: A Focus on Employability and Career Placement.* Springfield, Ill.: Charles C. Thomas, 1988.

A discussion of learning disabilities and suggestions for increasing the quality of employment for differently abled workers.

"Full Employment of People with Disabilities—A National Priority." *Fair Employment Practices.* Washington, D.C.: The Bureau of National Affairs, Inc., May 25, 1989, p. 66.

A discussion of the administration's commitment to removing barriers to employment of differently abled employees, including the Americans with Disabilities Act.

Fulwood, Sam. "Broad Disabled Rights Bill Okd." *Los Angeles Times*, May 23, 1990, p. A1.

A discussion of the Americans with Disabilities Act.

Nelson, Roberta. *Creating Acceptance for Handicapped People.* Springfield, Ill.: Charles C. Thomas, 1978.

A handbook for teaching the community to be supportive and accepting of people with physical and mental disabilities.

Nolan, Christopher. *Under the Eye of the Clock.* New York: St. Martin's Press, 1988.

Autobiography of a differently abled poet and writer.

Sagarin, Edward, ed. *The Other Minorities.* Waltham, Mass.: Xerox College Publishing, 1971, pp. 165–83.

A collection of articles focusing on nonethnic minorities such as differently abled people.

Spiegel, Allen D., and Simon Podair. *Rehabilitating People with Disabilities into the Mainstream of Society.* Park Ridge, N.J.: Noyes Medical Publications, 1981.

A collection of writings on the concerns of differently abled people, including a section on employment.

GENDER

Astrachan, Anthony. *How Men Feel.* New York: Anchor Press, 1988.
Discussion of how men feel about women, with a number of chapters on work relationships.

Barach, Grace, K.; Rosalind Barnett; and Caryl Rivers. *Lifeprints.* New York: McGraw-Hill, 1983.
A discussion of 1979–80 research on women's roles in the family, workplace, and society.

Cardwell, Len. "Managing Women—A Man's View." *Management Education and Development* 16, no. 2 (1985), pp. 197–200.
Article on the problems of male and female sexuality as they affect the workplace.

Collins, Glenn. "Men vs. Women at the Office." *New York Times,* January 30, 1987, p. A20.
Discussion of results of a study on sexual tension in the workplace.

Epperson, Sharon E. "Studies Link Subtle Sex Bias in Schools with Women's Behavior in the Workplace." *The Wall Street Journal,* September 16, 1988, p. 27.
Research on British and U.S. schools that shows differing teacher-pupil relationships depending on gender; consequences for the workplace.

Fernandez, John P. "New Life for Old Stereotypes." *Across the Board.* July/August 1988, pp. 24–29.
Discussion of results of extensive surveys on sexism and racism in the workplace.

Fierman, Jaclyn. "Why Women Still Don't Hit The Top." *Fortune,* July 30, 1990, p. 40.
A report on the continued obstacle of the glass ceiling in corporations and the experiences and sacrifices being made by women who break through it.

Gilligan, Carol. *In a Different Voice: Psychological Theory and Women's Development.* Cambridge, Mass.: Harvard University Press, 1962.
Discussion of gender differences in moral/ethical development, with implications for the workplace.

Giraldo, Zaida I. *Public Policy and the Family; Wives and Mothers in the Labor Force.* Lexington, Mass.: Lexington Books, 1980.
A discussion of mothers in the workplace, with implications for public policy and the family.

Gutek, Barbara A. *Sex and the Workplace.* San Francisco: Jossey-Bass, 1985.
A discussion of the impact of sexual behavior and harassment on

women, men, and organizations based on a study of 827 women and 405 men. Recommendations for managers.

Gutek, Barbara A. and Laurie Larwood, eds. *Women's Career Development.* Beverly Hills, Calif.: Sage Publications, 1986.
    A discussion of the psychological aspects of women's career development in the United States.
Gutek, Barbara A.; Bruce Morasch; and Aaron G. Cohen. "Interpreting Social-Sexual Behavior in a Work Setting." *Journal of Vocational Behavior* 22 (1983), pp. 30–48.
    A discussion of interpretations of ambiguous but potentially sexual behavior in the workplace.
Hardesty, Sarah, and Nehama Jacobs. *Success and Betrayal: The Crisis of Women in Corporate America.* New York: Franklin Watts, 1986.
    A discussion of the progress of professional women in corporate America.
Hochschild, Arlie. "Making It: Marginality and Obstacles to Minority Consciousness." In *Women and Success*, 2nd ed., ed. Ruth Kundsen, 1974, pp. 194–99.
    Discussion of women as a minority group and the alienation of corporate women from each other.
Hymowitz, Carol, and Timothy D. Schellhardt. "The Glass Ceiling: Why Women Can't Seem to Break the Invisible Barrier that Blocks Them from the Top Jobs." *The Wall Street Journal*, March 24, 1986, Sec. 4, p. 1.
    Summary of women managers' inability to reach upper-management eschelons and how the resulting frustration is sending them into entrepreneurial ventures.
Izraeli, Dafna N. "Sex Effects or Structural Effects? An Empirical Test of Kanter's Theory of Proportions." *Social Forces*, September 1983, pp. 153–65.
    Technical discussion of sex stereotypes, tokenism, and gender power differences.
Kanter, Rosabeth M. *Men and Women of the Corporation.* New York: Basic Books, 1977.
    Study of organizational behavior, with a focus on the rules of men and women and how they impact power relationships.
Kimmel, Michael S., ed. *Changing Men: New Directions in Research on Men and Masculinity.* Beverly Hills, Calif.: Sage Publications, 1987.
    An examination of recent research on men and masculinity.
Lipman-Blumen, Jean. *Gender Roles and Power.* Englewood Cliffs, N.J.: Prentice Hall, 1984.
    This book identifies and explains how the sex-gender system is a blueprint for all other power relationships.
Loden, Marilyn. *Feminine Leadership or How to Succeed in Business without Being One of the Boys.* New York: Times Books, 1985.
    Discussion of differences in male/female leadership styles and implicatins for enhancing the workplace.

Nkomo, Stella M., and Taylor Cox, Jr. "Gender Differences in the Upward Mobility of Black Managers: Double Whammy or Double Advantage." *Sex Roles* 21, no. 11 (1989).

Study of the career advancement of black men and women managers and a discussion of whether black women enjoy an advantage because of their gender.

McLoughlin, Merrill; T. Shryer; E. E. Goode; and K. McAuliffe. "Men vs. Women." *U.S. News and World Report*, August 8, 1988, pp. 50–57.

Summarizes research on physiological and psychological sex differences and the "gender gap."

Morrison, Ann M., and Mary Ann Von Glinow. "Women and Minorities in Management." *American Psychologist*, Feburary 1990, pp. 200–208.

Discussion of the current status of women and other minorities in upper management with an analysis of models that explain barriers to their advancement.

Morrison, Ann M.; Randall P. White; and Ellen van Velson. *Breaking the Glass Ceiling*. Reading, Mass: Addison-Wesley Publishing, 1987.

Discussion of factors that determine the success and failure of corporate women based on a study of executives.

Nieva, Veronica A., and Barbara Gutek. *Women and Work: A Psychological Perspective*. New York: Praeger Publishers, 1981.

Review of empirical and theoretical literature on the topic of women and work.

Powell, Gary. *Women and Men in Management*. Beverly Hills, Calif.: Sage Publications, 1988.

Comprehensive discussion of men and women at work; history, current research, and recommendations for change.

Rosener, Judy B. "Coping with Sexual Static." *New York Times Magazine*, December 7, 1986, p. 89.

Discussion of how sexual differences result in discomfort and confusion for women and men in the workplace.

Rosener, Judy B. "Confiscate the Gender Advantage." *Los Angeles Times*, April 1, 1989, Part II, p. 8.

Response to the "mommy track" argument.

Wallace, Phyliss A. *Black Women in the Labor Force*. Cambridge, Mass.: MIT Press, 1980.

A survey of economic literature on the employment status of black women.

RACE AND ETHNICITY

Allport, Gordon. *The Nature of Prejudice*. Reading, Mass.: Addison-Wesley Publishing, 1979.

A discussion about prejudices and antipathies.

Bell, Ella Louise. "Bicultural Life Experience of Career Oriented Black

Women," *Journal of Organizational Behavior*, Volume II, 1990.
A study examining the bicultural life of 71 black women who manage two cultural contexts: one black and one white.

Bergsman, Steve. "The Cycles of Identity." *Hispanic Business*. October 1989, p. 10.
Observations about Hispanics in business.

Brown, Dee. *Bury My Heart at Wounded Knee*. New York: Holt, Rinehart & Winston, 1970
A classic account of American Indian history.

Cox, Taylor, Jr., and Stella M. Nkomo., "Differential Performance Appraisal Criteria: A Field Study of Black and White Managers." *Group and Organization Studies* 11, no. 2 (March/June 1986).
Discussion of a study of the different ways in which the performance of black and white managers is evaluated.

Cox, Taylor Jr., and Stella M. Nkomo. "Invisible Men and Women: A Status Report on Race as a Variable in Organization Behavior Research." *Journal of Organizational Behavior*, Vol. 11, 1990.
Comprehensive compilation of research on people of color in the workplace.

Davis, George, and Glegg Watson. *Black Life in Corporate America*. Garden City, N.Y.: Doubleday, Anchor Press, 1982.
A discussion of the impact of mainstream organizational culture on black employees.

Farley, Reynolds. *Blacks and Whites: Narrowing the Gap?* Cambridge, Mass.: Harvard University Press, 1984.
A discussion of social trends in the United States with respect to African-Americans.

Fernandez, John. *Racism and Sexism in Corporate Life*. Lexington, Mass.: Lexington Books, 1981.
A discussion of the findings of a major study of black and white men and women and how racism and sexism affects their work life.

Hernandez, Carrol A.; Marcia J. Haug; and Nathaniel N. Wagner. *Chicanos*. St. Louis, Miss.: C. V. Mosby Company, 1976.
A discussion of Chicanos from a social and psychological perspective.

Hosokawa, Bill. *Nisei, The Quiet Americans*. New York: William Morrow, 1969.
A history of Japanese-Americans.

Katz, Judy H. *White Awareness: A Handbook for Anti-Racism*. Norman, Okla.: University of Oklahoma Press, 1978.
A discussion of racial discrimination, including psychological impacts and suggestions for group relations training.

Keefe, Susan E., and Amando Padilla. *Chicano Ethnicity*. Albuquerque, N.M.: University of New Mexico Press, 1987.
A discussion of Chicano ethnic loyalty and identity.

Kitano, Harry L., and Roger Daniels. *Asian Americans: Emerging Minorities*. Englewood Cliffs, N.J.: Prentice Hall, 1988.
A discussion of diverse Asian ethnic groups and their experiences.

Gary, Lawrence, ed. *Black Men*. Beverly Hills, Calif.: Sage Publications, 1981.
A discussion of contemporary issues that confront black men.

McCarthy, Cameron. "Rethinking Liberal and Radical Perspectives on Racial Inequality in Schooling: Making the Case for Nonsynchrony." *Harvard Educational Review*, August 1988, pp. 265–79.
Analysis of racial inequality in schooling.

Magnet, Myron. "Can Your Kid Become President?" *Fortune*. June 5, 1989, p. 271.
An article that suggests ethnicity is no longer a barrier to advancement in the United States.

Mirande, Alfredo. *The Chicano Experience: An Alternative Perspective*. Notre Dame: Ind.: University of Notre Dame Press, 1985.
A discussion of the social and economic conditions facing many Mexican-Americans.

Morin, Richard. "Fewer Whites Voicing Racial Bias: Poll Comparison Suggests Moderation of Attitudes toward Blacks." *The Washington Post*. October 26, 1989, p. A18.
An article that compares results of 1981 and 1989 *Washington Post*–ABC polls on race relations.

Rodgers-Rose, LaFrances. *Black Women*. Beverly Hills, Calif.: Sage Publications, 1983.
A discussion of issues that confront black women.

Ryan, William. *Blaming the Victim*. New York: Vintage Books, 1976.
A discussion of racial social conditions in the United States.

Sagarin, Edward, ed. "From the Ethnic Minorities to the Other Minorities." In *The Other Minorities*, ed. E. Sagarin. Waltham, Mass.: Xerox College Publishing, 1971, pp. 1–19.
Discussion of the characteristics of ethnic and nonethnic minority groups.

Schachter, Jim. "Unequal Opportunity: Minorities Find that Roadblocks to the Executive Suite are Still in Place." *Los Angeles Times*, April 17, 1988, p. 1.
Discussion of racial and sexual prejudices in the workplace.

Sowell, Thomas. *The Economics and Politics of Race: An International Perspective*. New York: William Morrow, 1983.
A cross-cultural study of economic and political aspects of race relations and ethnicity.

Tedlock, Dennis. *Teaching from the American Earth*. New York: Liveright, 1975.
A discussion of American Indian religion and philosophy.

White, Joseph L., and Thomas A. Parham. *The Psychology of Blacks: An African-American Perspective*. Englewood Cliffs, N.J.: Prentice Hall, 1990.
A comprehensive overview of the African-American experience in the United States.

Wilkerson, Isabel. "Study Finds Segregation in Cities Worse than Scientists Imagined." *New York Times*, August 5, 1989, p. 6.

Discussion of results of a demographic five-year study of segregation in 60 U.S. cities.

Work, John W. *Race, Economics, and Corporate America.* Wilmington, Del.: Scholarly Resources, Inc., 1984.
A discussion of socioeconomic factors and racist tendencies that influence the status of African-Americans.

SEXUAL/AFFECTIONAL ORIENTATION

Blumfeld, Warren, J., and Diane Raymond. *Looking at Gay and Lesbian Life.* Boston: Beacon Press, 1988.
A study of lesbian and gay lifestyles in the United States.

Kameny, Franklin, E. "Homosexuals as a Minority Group." In *The Other Minorities,* ed. E. Sagarin. Waltham, Mass.: Xerox College Publishing, 1971, pp. 50–65.
Discussion focusing on including gay men and lesbians as a minority group.

Katz, Jonathan. *Gay American History: Lesbians and Gay Men in the USA: A documentary.* New York: Thomas Y. Crowell, 1976.
A history of lesbians and gay men in the United States.

Leonard, Arthur S. "Gay and Lesbian Rights Protections in the U.S." Washington, D.C.: National Gay and Lesbian Task Force, 1989.
A compilation of municipalities and states with laws protecting lesbians and gay men in areas such as public employment, education, real estate and housing, credit, and others. Bias crime bills addressing anti-gay violence are also mentioned.

Libman, Gary. "Support Groups on the Job for Homosexuals." *Los Angeles Times,* July 18, 1990, p. E1.
A discussion of corporate support groups for lesbian and gay employees.

Pharr, Suzanne. *Homophobia: A Weapon of Sexism.* Inverness, Calif.: Chardon Press, 1988.
A discussion of heterosexism and sexism.

"Sharp Decline Found in Support for Legalizing Gay Relations." *The Gallup Report.* Report no. 254, November 1986.
Results of a survey on the acceptance of gay relationships and support for Supreme Court ruling against same-sex physical relations between consenting adults.

Index

A

Accounting firms, 133–34
Active cooperation in collusion, 116–17
Aetna Life and Casualty Company, 170–71
Affirmative action, 29–30, 174–75, 198–99
Age stereotypes, 65
Alvarez, Omar, 57
America West Airlines, 208
Apple Computers, 172
Assertion method, 96–97
Assimilation
  acknowledging limits of, 143–44
  and cultural diversity, 37–38
  versus diversity, 34–35
  failure of, 140–41, 219
  to homogeneous culture, 42–44
  impact on diverse employees, 44–49
  impact on dominant group, 49–53
  myth, 139–40
  rationales for, 137–38
  reinforcement, 37–42
Authority base, 92–93
Avoidance, 124
Awareness education, 151–56
  basic elements, 202–4
  need for, 187–89
  organizational priority, 171–73

B

Baby bust, 7–8
Bass, Alison, 79 n
Bennett, Amanda, 179 n
Bennis, Warren G., 180, 194 n
Berg, Eric C., 136 n
Berman, Melissa A., 79 n
Business
  assimilation versus diversity, 34–35
  civil rights law enforcement, 29–31
  creating culture of diversity, 196–215
  homogeneous culture control, 36–37
  integrated, 141–42

Business—*Cont.*
  leading-edge organizations, 160–78
  pluralistic leadership, 180–94
  steps to integration, 139–50
  structures supporting change, 209–11
  suppression of support groups, 41–42
  values of white males, 28–39
Business-as-usual attitude, 220–21
Business Week, 122
Butler, Lee, 118 n

C

Candor, 110–11
Career development seminars, 172
Certified public accountants, 133–34
Change
  education and, 202–13
  openness to, 189–90
Civil Rights Act of 1964, 125, 126, 177
Civil rights legislation, 29–31
Coaching mechanisms, 212–13
Collaborative alliances, 149
Collusion
  active cooperation in, 116–17
  breaking pattern of, 117–18
  denial, 115–16
  nature of, 111–12
  origins, 112–13
  silence, 114–15
  and stereotyping, 113–17
  survival strategy, 113
Common ground
  definition, 138–39
  derailment issues, 150–56
  initiatives toward, 142–50
  myth versus reality, 139–40
  paths to, 140–41
Communication
  closed networks, 46
  decoding, 99–102
  diverse styles, 86–87
  dominant group problems, 80–82
  elements of style, 87–90
  language sensitivity, 82–86

245